TAUGHT BY
DOGS

*For all those dogs to whom the human race
should have been nicer.
And, of course, for Chris, who has earned
the unreserved love of all our dogs.*

TAUGHT BY
DOGS

COLIN WHITTEMORE

MERLIN UNWIN BOOKS

First published in Great Britain by Merlin Unwin Books Ltd 2024

Merlin Unwin Books
6 Rural Enterprise Centre
Eco Park Road
Ludlow
SY8 1FF

www.merlinunwin.co.uk

ISBN 978 1 913159 78 8

Typeset in Adobe Caslon Pro 12pt by Joanne Dovey,
Merlin Unwin Books

Printed by CPI Anthony Rowe England

Contents

About the Author

Colin Whittemore was raised on a small family farm in Cheshire near the Welsh Borders and has continued to work with animals all his life. His love of dogs began on the farm and eventually led to a career in animal science and well-being. He is Emeritus Professor at the University of Edinburgh and has been awarded the Royal Agricultural Society Gold Medal for outstanding research in agriculture. Author of several countryside books, he continues to write about farming and the countryside. He tends his natural wildflower meadow in the Scottish Borders where he enjoys long walks with his dog. He lives in West Linton with his wife, Chris.

Prologue

In our old age, the household has become very different. In its heyday the place was full of life, noise and expectation. The family had progressively outgrown the house we started with. With the arrival of our third child it became obvious that the kitchen could no longer hold the muddy boots, the wet clothes and the two dog beds, as well as the guinea pig's cage, the canary, and everything else that was lugged in (including the rabbit hutch) whenever there was a nip in the air.

We had needed an extension. One with a utility room. No sooner was this added on to the back kitchen door, than it was filled, maybe because a third puppy had arrived out of the blue, courtesy of a reckless visit by mother and daughter to the dog and cat refuge.

Come to think of it, the change in the household today is not so much a matter of the four children leaving the family home as a matter of my wife and I becoming for one more time in our lives, a *ménage à trois*.

Us two, and our small dog, Rufus, just the three of us. Rufus has to fill an awful lot of those empty spaces left by absence of children and the passing of all those dogs that were his predecessors. The mud on the floors, the disturbed nights and early morning wake-ups, the noisy interruptions, the misbehaviour, and of course the play times. All of which, and more, he achieves admirably. But mostly Rufus is busy being a dog, doing dog things, which is what dogs do best of all. And this is quite enough, bless him. We would be bereft without our little dog.

There are ghosts in this house. Memories of many dogs, all happy ghosts. Ghosts we are pleased to have around.

The loss of a dog is a hard thing to bear: but being without a dog is *impossible* to bear.

We decided that we would bring Rufus home because we had come to the realisation that for a house to be a home there has to be a dog. We could not be a family without a dog. That was always the case but it is only now, with Rufus, that the realisation has fully dawned.

That was what had been so awful about boarding school – there were no dogs there. It's how the old people's home is going to be, I guess…

*****

Our first family dog, little Brandy – a Norwich terrier – was thrust upon us, when we were a 'young married couple' as they used to say. We were not willing recipients. We had decided that we postively did not want, were in no position to have, a dog of any sort. Brandy came from my family's farm and it was they who decided we needed to be presented with a puppy.

The family farm was never short of terriers about the place. All small dairy farms are natural havens for any number of them, usually Jack Russell mongrels, but in Brandy's case pure-bred because her mother was one of a new breed of dog to be found on our farm – one that was destined to live in the house, not the barn. Brandy's mother was a pet dog on the farm, not a working dog.

A pet dog was quite a novel concept. At first, I could not understand what Brandy's mother, Samatha, was *for*. 'Dog' when I was a boy had been synonymous with 'working dog'. Dogs were farm animals, either for herding or for hunting. Brandy was to be neither, she was our companion – a family dog.

My earlier life with dogs had been inevitably and firmly rooted in the farm where I was raised but left as a young man. It is proper therefore that the story of our dogs begins on the farm with the many critters which shared their rural lives with us kids.

Mother had her hounds, Father had his sheepdogs and the farm had its terriers.

On a small family farm, the farmhouse is not a separate dwelling distinct from the animal buildings. The farmhouse is a built-in part of the farmyard, constructed no differently from the cart shed or the cow byre. As kids we did not go from the 'house' to the 'farm'. In the house we were already on the farm; it was a matter of moving between two parts of the same whole – and without always changing our boots in between either! The dogs saw it that way too.

That is why farm dogs – even those living in the farmhouse – are different from family companion dogs. My good fortune has been to have known both.

Perhaps then, I should start on the farm.

Father's Sheepdogs

Most of our sheepdogs on the farm where I was brought up in the 1940s and 1950s came from 'Uncle' Bert Wright. He had a reputation for training sheepdogs. The best ones he kept for himself or sold to the hill shepherds in Snowdonia. The others he got rid of to the Cheshire dairy farmers as cattle dogs. They were good enough for that job. We had a herd of Dairy Shorthorns.

There is a fascination in watching sheepdogs at work. It is not just that they are clever, nor that they are working (not playing). It is that they are so obviously planning ahead. They can see already what we have yet to see – they know what is *about* to happen.

If truth be told, the nearest I ever saw Father get to handling sheepdogs was him watching – in his dotage – Phil Drabble's TV series *One Man and his Dog*. He was in admiration and envy of the men (it was only men) who could command their dogs with nothing more than a whistle, to round up and pen a flock of sheep.

Dad had a sheepdog whistle made of bent metal – a flat half-circle with a single hole in the middle of it. Only proper shepherds could ever get a sound out of these things, but Father managed it rather well. He even took to making these whistles and giving them away to the shepherds of north Wales at the agricultural shows we took our dairy cows to. We always did well with our Dairy Shorthorns at the shows. Pity they never produced enough milk to clear a profit!

Although there were no sheep on our farm, there were always some of Uncle Bert's Welsh sheepdogs. These were working dogs, tools of the trade for herding the cattle, bringing them in from the fields for the early morning and late afternoon milkings. One sees Welsh collies urging sheep to break into a run, but our dogs never ever caused a cow to make any greater pace than a gentle amble. Running was not something either the dairyman nor the cow would ever want.

There were always two sheepdogs on our farmyard (or three if a puppy was coming on). One would be chained outside with a kennel to sleep in, usually an old beer-barrel on its side which we kept from rolling with chocks of wood. This dog was there to be unleashed for work at a moment's notice. He would only run free when he was working: to fetch the cattle in, then throughout the twice-daily milkings to keep the cows in order while they loafed about waiting to be milked and finally, to return the cows to their grazing pasture.

The other dog was cleaner in its coat and sweeter in its smell. This one lived in the farm kitchen, and was allowed to come into the dining area to curl up and lie by the fire. This too was a working dog, but one that was also part of the family – Father's dog.

Uncle Bert was a mate of Father's who farmed Kerry sheep on land neighbouring ours. They would share a pint or two at the Boat Inn. Bert would always come down to the pub with his sheepdog. Unbidden, unleashed and undirected, the dog would follow at his heel, waiting at the bar until the pint was put on to the counter. At that he would lead the way to the dark oaken chair in which his master always sat, to curl up underneath. Not to sleep, for the dog never slept, but to be ready, when three pints had been downed and the Innkeeper bid goodnight, to be up and lead his master to the door and back home.

This, you will understand, was not one special dog. The whole succession of a shepherd's dogs over the years behaved the same. They were all trained the same, and all worked the sheep the same. They were working dogs, trained by the same master.

Father was hugely impressed by the bond between Uncle Bert and his dog. As a result he forever tried to get our own dogs to curl up under his chair at the table-end while he was at his breakfast, dinner or tea. But none of them ever would. He was both cross and saddened that the house dog did not pay proper respect to him as head of the household. But dogs are blind to a rank that is given. Dogs see only the rank that is *earned*. If the house sheepdog was ever under anybody's chair, they were under Mother's. That didn't much please Father either.

The shepherd in this case owned fields of his own and rented more round about. Because of his friendship with Father, I was to call him 'Uncle' Bert. Uncle Bert kept sheep and dealt in both sheep and cattle at the local markets. He bought young stock to sell on to other farmers and he also sold their finished beef cattle and their lambs to the local butchers.

He had a little house down in the village with a beautiful cottage garden all around it kept by his diminutive Welsh-speaking wife. I was invited into their house once for a cup of tea. Even though Uncle Bert was a farmer, his house was not at all like ours. His house was clean, clean as a new pin. It was the neatest, shiniest place I had seen – or was ever likely to. Mrs Bert was a cause of wonderment to us all. She made a great cup of tea served with scones which, in the hunger years after the war, were unmatched in the parish.

Bert Wright was a rich man, or so it was understood. He was a clever dealer, much respected for his honest trading. He was also feared, because he could make a fellow farmer his fortune or render him penniless. Uncle Bert was the deal-maker of the local market trade. He was shrewd. His speed and ability with numbers were legendary yet he never ever used a notebook or pencil. It was all done in his head.

At my father's bidding when I was around eight or nine years old I would accompany Uncle Bert to the markets at Mold and Wrexham on two days a week. I had a job to do.

When Uncle Bert was selling I had to be sure to note who had bought what and for how much. I would then make out a paper record to that effect. This Bert Wright would sign before I was to give it to the various buyers, together with the luck money. The next part of that job was to be the courier in charge of the cheque that was to be made out to 'Albert Wright Esq.' It was my job to be sure that everything was made out correctly.

When Uncle Bert was buying, I was in charge of his chequebook. I wrote out all the cheques in pounds, shillings and pence, with the payee's name properly spelled. Then, as for the invoice, Bert Wright would add his signature at the bottom. If I remember correctly, I had to lick a tuppenny stamp and stick it on. Uncle Bert had a strange signature, which I never questioned. It was an 'X'. A rather fancy X, it has to be said, but an X all the same.

Some years later, at Bert Wright's funeral, I found myself talking to one of the local farmers who knew him well. I recounted my experiences with Uncle Bert as a youngster at the local markets, commenting on the strange signature.

'Goodness me boy, did you not realise why you had that job? Albert Wright could neither read nor write, nor could he scribe a single word on a piece of paper. Somebody else always had to do that.'

Nobody tried to diddle Bert Wright, it would not have been worth their while.

Uncle Bert's ability to work the markets was exceptional, but his other persona – that of shepherd – was not. Farming as we did on the north Wales borders, we were surrounded by shepherds, and they were all equal masters with their dogs. The dogs were their livelihood. The Welsh collie dog to the shepherd was as the gun to the gamekeeper; the tool of his trade. Just as the gamekeeper must have mastery of his gun, so must the shepherd be the master of his dog.

I have no recollection of much trade in fully trained sheepdogs for sale to the Welsh shepherds themselves. Youngsters were traded, yes; but ready-made dogs, no. The dogs had their natural instinct to round up stock. Herding was written through their genes. The rest was up to its owner to train the puppy both in unquestioning obedience to command *and* in the ability to think for themselves when no command was forthcoming. Artistry is required on the part of the shepherd; when to command and when to leave a wise dog to it. Most shepherds trained their own dogs. It was a matter of pride, but it was also a matter of normal expectation. A shepherd was as good as his dog.

There was only one way to put obedience into an ever-flighty Welsh sheepdog, and that was with a justified reward. There were two schools of practice (not schools of thought; it was never a matter for thinking, it was a matter of *doing*). The first was to praise when right was done and to offer silent disdain when it was not. The second way of training was to reward with silence, but to chastise error with harsh words or physical violence. In the first case the dog could bask in the sunlight of being told that they had done well. In the second case the dog only knew of the darkness of scolding when they had done wrong.

Both methods seemed to work equally well. Which was a pity really. But these animals were not pets.

*****

My Uncle Arthur was a most gifted schoolteacher of mathematics. For this he had no qualification other than his RAF Navigation training as a Pilot Officer (Air/Sea Rescue) in the early years of World War II. But before being a schoolteacher, he had been a singularly ungifted farmer.

Aunty Beryl and Uncle Arthur farmed in the hilly countryside of Denbigh. She hated it. A sophisticated town girl, she had to learn to live by the light of a paraffin Tilly lamp, with water from a well, and heat from open coal (best Welsh) fires, which did nothing to lessen the all-pervading damp.

Being a dairy farm, they naturally needed a Welsh sheepdog to bring the herd in from the pastures for twice-daily milking. Naturally, they got their dogs from the local shepherds. Naturally, these were the cast-offs that the canny locals had determined would never 'make'. Or, put more simply, were useless at herding anything – not even the farmyard ducks.

Uncle Arthur's dog was big for a Welsh collie, and lived his useless life in front of the kitchen fire, the kitchen being the only warm room in the house. I have no recollection of this animal's name, but I do remember being amazed at the one singular skill he had. He excelled at playing.

This was a revelation to me as a ten-year-old. I had never ever come across a dog with whom people played. Aunty Beryl, doubtless to give some relief to her arduous and unsought lifestyle, had taught the dog to run after sticks, and catch them high in the air. This was quite amazing to me, though perhaps a little undignified for a Welsh collie.

The thing was, I had never seen a dog play, let alone actually played with a dog myself. Dogs were for working, not playing. Gathering sheep, herding cattle, retrieving shot pigeons, following the scent of fox or hare, chasing the farm cats, killing rats, guarding the steading against marauding gypsies and other such ne'er-do-wells. But never playing.

As I was happy to help milk the cows but less happy to clean the shippon out afterwards, a day at Uncle Arthur's could get tedious. Thus it must have been that, exasperated, Aunty Beryl sent me out of the house 'to play with the dog', which I did, much to my, and I hope the dog's, great delight. However high or far that stick was thrown, it would always be caught by the dog up in mid-air, leaping high off the muddy ground. Such fun. But only ever at Uncle Arthur's. Never anywhere or anytime else.

Dogs were to be gainfully employed. They were, above all, not playthings, not toys.

*****

Whilst at Agricultural College, my Easter vacations (and one summer one too) was spent shepherding on Glyder Fach and Glyder Fawr, part of the Snowdonia range. The farm, Dyffryn Mymbyr (valley of the river), was intimidating both in respect to its rugged landscape and its ancient farmhouse (now with the National Trust). Dyffryn farm was intimidating due to its owner, the legendary Esmé Firbank. Esmé had been swept off her feet by Thomas Firbank and taken to the mountain he had just bought in the romantic belief that he wanted to be a sheep farmer. Having established himself and his wife there, he concluded he no longer wanted either wife or farm and pushed off, leaving both Esmé and mountain to their own devices. Esmé was a diminutive woman determined to show the local farmers and shepherds that she was their equal; well up to their mettle. She more than succeeded in that. She was fearsome! However, Esmé herself notwithstanding, more intimidating even than her was her Dyffryn shepherd.

His four Welsh sheepdogs lived in an outbuilding at the back of the big house. They would await his appearance as soon as dawn was breaking. The dogs would go wild with delight upon sighting him in the light of the old farmhouse kitchen door. It was from here that he would emerge after finishing his breakfast and stuffing his lunch into his jacket pocket.

This love match was one hundred percent one-sided. The dogs loved the shepherd. The shepherd did not love the dogs. He loved the already spoken-for young lady at the other end of the Gyrhyd valley.

The dogs were what he needed for his work. He neither loved nor hated his work. It was what he did, that was all. If the dogs worked well, he did his work well, which pleased him. If his day of toil did not go well, it was the dogs' fault so they got cursed for it. Cursed in the native Welsh language (a very good language for delivering curses); cursed at length; cursed at full volume.

I might be expected to manage some sort of adequate description of these four dogs, but I cannot. They were black and white Welsh sheepdogs. They will have had names to be sure, Welsh names, with the consequence that the dog's name being called was likely to sound to me as incomprehensible as to the dog being sworn at. They were dirty with muck and mud, a breed characteristic. They smelt awful – another breed characteristic. Apart from that, they were the shepherd's dogs and that was that. Come twenty years earlier or twenty years later, they would all have been just the same.

The Dyffryn shepherd was not into complimentary remarks; not to his dogs, not to his employer, not to me. Indeed, he was not much into remarks of any sort; his words were few, and mostly derogatory. For some reason though, like the dogs, I was content enough to work with him. He knew what he was about and I trusted him.

On a normal day in the spring he would strike up the hill with his dogs alongside. He never had a vehicle of any description. He had no need. He would go up the hill on foot like a Snowdonian feral goat. Straight up. My own route up the hill would be a zig-zag, like any normal being, traversing back and forth to lessen the slope. He would be out of sight over the lower slopes of the Glyder before I had barely got started from the farm steading.

The day would be spent walking the hill to check the sheep. Most of them stayed hefted up on the heights, even through the lambing season. Only the youngsters were brought down to the Ffridd nearer the farm so their actual lambing could be attended if need arose (which was not often).

The main problem around lambing was in the last seven-to-ten days of the pregnancy when a fair few of them would go down, falling comatose. The only treatment to stave off a dead ewe (another carcass left to lie out for the raptors) was an injection of calcium borogluconate. Its effects were immediate and magical. Instead of expiring, the ewes would jump up and stagger off. My own equipment while walking the hills was a big syringe and two large bottles of magic muti. I carried a crook as well, but that was rarely needed. Any sheep I spotted as needing my ministering were already down and on the way out. I, of course, did not have the benefit of a dog.

These Welsh mountain sheep rarely had twins; singles were the rule. Any ewe up the mountain looking like needing help with delivering its lamb would be cornered by the dogs for the shepherd to grab her to render the necessary assistance.

At the end of the day the dogs were fed on slops of offal and meal – there were always dead sheep carcasses about the place awaiting to be to skinned and jointed. Then the dogs were shut up in the slum at the back of the farmhouse to curl up, sleep, and await the next dawn that would bring their release.

*****

It was at Gathering time that the dogs came into their own. Gathering the sheep from the hills where they lived their lives was a fairly regular occurrence, though that did not make a gathering any less of an occasion for the shepherds or less challenging for the dogs. For at least half the Gatherings, the neighbouring farms would cooperate together so that all the local hillsides were cleared and the flocks brought down on the same day (or two days). The purpose of this was so that the sheep that had strayed from their hefts and were uninvited guests of the next-door farm could be picked out to be returned back to their rightful territories. Every ewe was branded with the farm's special mark.

At a big Gathering there could be a dozen dogs up the hills of Glyder Fawr (the big one), Glyder Fach (the small one, a few feet lower) and Tryfan (the one with three rocky tops). The dogs would be taken part way up, then be sent off. They would soon be out of hearing, then fade from sight. You could track them for a while as they lost their black and white shapes and became mere shades moving across the rough grasses, rocks and heather. Then they were gone. The shepherds would stand about down below. Silent. Watchful. The wait seemed endless. The dogs had gone off into the wilderness, seemingly never to return.

Then the shepherds would begin to shift and move, long before you could see why. What they had spied – and you had not – were the first grey specks, way up above, making their way slowly down the hill. As soon as the little flecks of white began to form into grey streams of sheep, the men would know just where the flocks would be coming down. Thus directed, they would strike off with long deliberate strides up the hill. They too would cover the ground with breathtaking speed to gain ground and height to help their dogs marshal the sheep on, downwards into the pens at the steading.

The wonder of it all was that the whole operation was carried out by the dogs working amongst themselves and without instruction. I developed a deep respect for these dogs – more so than for their masters.

The main Gatherings were for shearing and for the Grand Autumn Sale. The dogs were just as essential to getting the sheep into the pens down at the farm buildings, as to getting them off the hill in the first place. They marshalled the sheep into the shearer's hands and then, after clipping, away into the holding pens. They just got on and did this, jumping about all the while on and off the dry-stone walls, bossing the sheep.

The Dyffryn sale was a tremendous occasion for the north Wales farmers who would come from far and wide to buy. Up for sale first were the young Welsh Black beef stock that would go to be fattened out on lower pastures for selling the next year as finest Black beef. Then came the cull ewes that were too old for another winter on the hill, but good for another couple of seasons in the softer climes of the Welsh Marches where, put to a Suffolk ram, they would rear twins.

Most of all however, the purpose of the Dyffryn sales were to get shut of the lambs. Esmé Firbank did not like taking her stock to the lottery of the farmers' livestock markets. Half the season's lambs would be the males, ripe for fattening on lowland pastures ready before Christmas as prime Welsh lamb to be exported to England. The other half, the females, were halved again. A quarter of the crop would be sold as hardy breeding stock to upland farmers for crossing with a Leicester ram; while the remaining quarter would be kept back for replenishing the Dyffryn flock – to return to the heft where they were born, up the slopes of the Glyder.

At the autumn sale it wasn't just the sheep that were gathered at Dyffryn Mymbyr. The farmers were too. They would have started the day early, to come to the far reaches of the Snowdonia hills. They would return late home. So naturally, they all brought their sheepdogs with them. This was normal. Opening the door of the Land Rover of a morning was an open invitation to the farm dogs to leap in the back, there to ride with their heads stuck out into the slip stream. There would be more dogs at the sale than people!

*****

In years previous I had simply taken for granted the Welsh sheepdog's natural intelligence and ability to 'read' the actions of other animals. They were just sheepdogs. That's the way they were. Welsh sheepdogs can see ahead, they can plan, they can foresee a situation and map instantly what will happen next.

A sheepdog will 'go the wrong way' to cut off an escaping quarry. They will warn of impending disaster before any human is aware of the danger.

From an early age, we boys would take off from the farmhouse and be gone for most of a day roaming the countryside around.

'We're away off up the fields, Mum.'

'Then take the dog. Keep him with you.'

It was always, 'Take the dog'. We could not understand this for a long while; the sheepdogs were hardly in need of the exercise! The fact of it was that Mother trusted the dog to look after us. He would bark at us if we climbed too high in the trees after birds' nests. He would dash about at the pond's edge when we ventured out too far across the thin ice. But he would also join joyously in our rabbit catching and coot-hunting – both requiring the active participation of the sheepdogs.

The coots we would flush out of the reeds and onto open water where they would be bombarded with stones from our catapults. This would cause them to dive. With repeated diving they would run short of oxygen, taking to the bank – where the dogs would be eagerly waiting. We ate the coots – casseroled.

We casseroled the rabbits too. The technique for catching them was rather similar to that for the coots. The ferrets were put down into the rabbit warrens. After a pause laden with anticipation – on the part of both children and dogs – the rabbits would hurtle out of their escape holes. Sharp-eyed, the dogs were ready. The chase over open ground was usually short... very short if Rowan the Wolfhound was on hand.

*****

Sheepdogs, ferrets and guns were inextricably bound together in the lives of us farm boys. The ferrets (two hob polecats and one little white jill) lived in a hutch hidden at the back of the hen house – in the least salubrious part of what was already a pretty dirty and smelly quarter of the farmyard. The execrable foxhound puppies were housed close by!

The ferrets were fed intermittently, as would be natural for their species in the wild; and as would be natural for any beast put into the care of irresponsible young farm lads.

They lived mostly off dead, or nearly dead, chickens which were too far gone even for Mother to demand that they were plucked, dressed and boiled for our dinner. The ferrets were appreciative of their provender coming along immediately the poor hen's necks were wrung and they were flung unceremoniously into the ferret-house.

The ferrets liked to feed off the blood and offal before beginning the longer-term job of dealing with the meat and bone. The jill would take comfort in living inside the cavity of the chicken carcass, while it was being demolished over the period of the next week or so – in which task, the ferrets would be assisted by the flies and the ensuing maggots. In the best interests of what would now be called 'recycling sustainability', the maggots in turn would be extracted from the morass to be employed by us boys as fishing bait.

Despite the stink that clung stubbornly to the ferrets' rich fur coats, we eschewed the wooden 'ferret-box' for transportation while out hunting rabbits. The ferrets were simply tucked inside our shirts and lived curled around that nook that separates the bottom of the human rib-cage from the top of the thigh bone. Extracting them from thence to put them to work could be tricky if the ferret took exception to a probing hand!

Traditionally, the sport of ferreting for rabbit meat required the accompaniment of not so much sheepdogs as a dozen or so small string nets. These were spread over the exit holes of the rabbit warren and pegged securely. Alarmed by the presence of a (very smelly) ferret introduced into their home and on the hunt for blood, the terrified bunnies would bolt their burrow, hit the net and entrap themselves – secured by the peg until they were hit forcibly with the side of the hand on the back of their necks. These were the best ones for the stew-pot (for reasons that will become evident), and were skinned and gutted on the spot. The guts were placed at the entrance holes of the rabbit warren, thus to tempt the ferret out of the warren, ready for the next foray.

However, netting was dull sport for us boys as well as for the sheepdogs. The dogs had no opportunity for an overground chase unspoilt by their quarry resorting to unsporting behaviour, such as disappearing into a hole in the ground.

So, as often as not, the nets were never put out.

Bolting rabbits, flushed from their homes by the ferrets, would appear at speed from one or other of their exit holes and hurl themselves across open ground, joyfully pursued by a riot of over-excited dogs.

Above all things, our sheepdogs loved a chase. There was always some chance that the rabbit would escape, which to us seemed fair enough and it was great fun for all concerned.

My elder brother rather fancied himself first with catapult and then, having reached the age of firearm responsibility (ten years old), with shot-gun. This element of the sport was rather more beset with hazard than either netting or pursuit by dog. The escaping rabbit would normally have a number of choices of hole to bolt from. Thus the aspirant marksman would have to react quickly to the brown blur that could come from any quarter. It is a wonder that none of the dogs, nor any of the ferrets, ended up being shot. But they never did.

Mother, however, was not enamoured with these latter, more exciting, versions of the sport, as the skinned carcass presented to her for the pot would invariably be peppered with lead-shot, bruised by dog incisor teeth, or both.

A downside of a day's ferreting was the time spent waiting for the ferret, having been sent so willingly down the hole, to decide that it might deign to come out again. Rabbit warrens could be, well, warrens; with many passages and turns. If a kill was made underground, the ferret would (especially if the last dead hen had been some time previous) enjoy a leisurely lunch, perhaps followed by an after-dinner snooze and even a little tea upon wakening.

To address this most serious shortcoming in the sport of ferreting, a collar could be put upon the ferret (the polecats, having bigger heads, were best for this) and a string line attached. At every yard, a knot was put in the line; one knot, then two knots, then three etc. This way the distance into the warren travelled by the ferret could be determined. It was tempting to try to drag the ferret out of the burrow, but this invariably failed as upon sensing the line tighten, the polecat would lock onto his kill, thus requiring not one body but two to be hauled out. As rabbit warrens have many corners, this was invariably fruitless. Standard practice was to dig the ferret out with a hand spade, following the run of the line. This could be a lengthy and arduous task, but often rewarded not only by the retrieving of a well-loved ferret, but also by the finding of more than one rabbit cornered into a deep-down dead-end.

It became fashionable to muzzle the ferrets, fastening tight shut the ferret's jaws so they could not kill when in the warren. This ensured all rabbits were flushed into the nets in good order for cooking, to be followed in due course by the ferret who, having made no kill, would himself seek to exit.

We tried this a few times, but upon losing an albino hob ferret, we gave up on it. We had abandoned the poor beast to his fate, which would be, as Father pointed out starkly when we got home, slow starvation.

The best fun on offer, especially for the sheepdogs, remained the dog chase. There was nothing better, we boys concluded, than to watch a mixed pack of yelping dogs charge helter-skelter about the field after a rabbit jinking in full flight. These were exciting moments, regrettably scarcely available to any youngster in the present day, even those few left living in the countryside.

Is that because modern youth is more civilised? No evidence there! Besides, we took our bounty home and it ended up on the supper table.

And we were hungry children.

*****

Sometimes one of our favourite sheepdog companions, Rap – an important and lively member of the gang – would disappear from our company. Rap was clearly under orders from Mother to keep an eye on us. We had cause on occasion to be grateful for his absconding: once when I had fallen from a tree and was unconscious at its base; and another time when we decided that it would be fun to see if a leaky old row-boat would get all the way across a large pond, with us boys on board! On both occasions Rap had reappeared with Mother in tow. Brought there by Rap to rescue her errant offspring! But it was rare indeed that we kids ever did anything without the accompaniment of the family sheepdog.

However, not all our sheepdogs were super intelligent, do-no-wrong, good and faithful servants. Peg was not a clever dog. She would watch the other dogs when we were cooting or rabbiting, never sure what to do and generally getting in the way. She was useless at bringing in the cows; never really got the hang of it.

She had a tail that was so strong that it wagged her whole back end. She was forever yawning, craving praise and asking to be patted in a most unprofessional way. But she was a kindly dog.

Like most of our dogs, Peg just seemed to appear as a young pup to join the mêlée at the farm. Having another dog with us was no great agony of decision-making – not like the sort that happens these days before a puppy is brought into a modern household as a pet. One more dog about the farm and farmhouse was neither here nor there.

The usual count of dogs on the farm was: four in the house (sheepdog, terriers, hound), two or three working dogs out in kennels or running free on the yard, and – for a part of the year – three foxhound puppies. Then of course to that would be added any dogs that the farm workers had with them – invariably terriers.

Peggy got away with her lack of talent for quite a while. The dairy cows assumed that she, being a sheepdog, would operate just like all the others had done. So when Peg hove into view, wagging her tail, dodging enthusiastically and aimlessly about, the herd would give her (undeserved) respect.

'Heads-up girls: Pay attention: Best be getting together and off down to milking,' or 'Here's the dog: Let's be off before we're chased: Get back up to that pasture: Best we behave.'

But as time went by the cattle got wise to the fact that Peg's strange antics were not super cleverness, but super stupidity. With Peggy about, disobedient behaviour on the cows' part went unchecked, and was soon the norm. The herd became unruly. Cows would be charging about the place, fences broken, cornfields trampled. Poor Peggy was more hindrance than help.

She would have to go.

The dog's extremes of friendliness and enthusiasm and her excessive tail-wagging were however Peggy's salvation in the end. A frequent visitor to the yard was the cattle-feed salesman – whose name was Parker. We actually called *him* Peggy (but never in his hearing – he was a nice man). The salesman and the dog were two of the same kind, both constantly seeking approval, smiling through adversity, totally hopeless at their jobs. Peg had cantered onto the yard the moment she heard Parker's car. A mutually effusive welcome ensued, with much licking of faces. Ever attentive to a customer's requirements, Parker listened with vigorous head nodding to our bewailing about the uselessness of the dog.

'What you going to do with her then?'

'Don't know. She's useless at everything. She's even useless at being useless.'

'I'll have her!'

'Eh?'

'I'll have her. The Mrs has always wanted a sheepdog. She'll just love her.' 'Here Peg! Here Peggy!' Peggy came, tail wagging as ever. Open any car door and you can depend upon a sheepdog to jump in.

Problem solved.

*****

My elder brother must have been in his early teens when he acquired the first dog he could call his own. I do not remember him as being much of a doggy person although he definitely had little love for other animals. He avoided the dairy cattle, ignored the hens, despised the pigs. My brother was into machines: the bigger the better – tractors, diggers, drainers, bull-dozers. His other enthusiasm was for shooting. Pigeons, sparrows, cats, rabbits and most everything else that moved, he shot at with deadly accuracy. First with a murderously effective catapult, then a rather powerful airgun, next a four-ten shotgun, then a rather nice double-barrelled twelve-bore.

These weapons were aired on occasional forays out into a cowering countryside along with a revolver pistol (never hit anything), or a wicked .22 Winchester pump-action repeater rifle which combined (still does) accuracy with range. I must not condemn; these same things were not only normal agricultural activities for farm boys, they were also 'pastimes' to which I myself aspired. I was never as good a shot as he was, however. My own blood-sport was foxhunting – more animal orientated – the horses and the hounds.

My brother's dog was not pure Welsh sheepdog. It wasn't clear what had got at his mother, but the puppies had big patches of telltale red in their coats. His name was Gilpin. Gilpin was a canny dog. He never showed much affection for any of us with, for no obvious reason, the singular exception of my brother. Maybe he liked the hunting expeditions with the gun. Gilpin would always take himself off with my brother whenever he left the yard with catapult in his hand, or later, a gun under his arm. Despite my brother's usual antipathy to animals, the two of them just hit it off. They became inseparable and everywhere that one would go, the other would be with him. They thought the world of each other.

At the extreme corner of the farm was a wood, a favourite haunt of foxes (below ground) and pigeons (above). Unbeknownst to my brother who was within the wood waiting on a flock of pigeons to come in to roost, the neighbouring farmer's boy was out with his own gun looking for foxes to shoot. Gilpin, messing about in the undergrowth, put up a fox which broke cover and Gilpin (as was his way) gave chase. Our neighbour's lad saw two 'foxes' glinting red break from the wood out into the open field and shot dead the second one. The nearest one. The bigger one.

My brother never recovered from that loss. Not least because his best mate had been shot in front of his eyes. He never had any other dog that he called his own. Nor did he have quite the same appetite any more for the sport of shooting.

*****

The last sheepdog on the old family farm was an overweight Welsh bitch we called Bessie. She was still young when we finally got rid of the Dairy Shorthorn herd, so she ran out of work. The Shorthorns were pretty to look at, but in the twenty years we had the herd, they had turned in a profit only twice! With the cows gone, Bessie would amuse herself with the pigs which were still turned out into the paddocks through the day. But soon they too would be ushered into the new ways of farming, to be kept inside all the time in purpose-built pig-houses.

Bessie was the yard dog, not a house dog. She grew fat and lazy. Without work to do she became first agitated, then snappy, then neurotic. She was not a happy sheepdog. She was the last dog to survive on our traditional family farm. Things would be different from now on. Dad went and got the .22 and Bessie was put down. The end of an era.

The Welsh sheepdogs were always seen as belonging to Father, which was strictly correct, for the dogs were down on the books as 'farm livestock/farm equipment' together with the Shorthorn dairy cows, the Yorkshire pigs, and the Fordson tractors. Dad it was who got them from Uncle Bert, I'm sure. But not one single sheepdog was ever truly his. To own a sheepdog you must work and play together, go through thick and thin together, share the day with all its joys and knocks together.

Oh! And be the one that feeds it.

Mother's Hounds

I suppose we two boys were around ten years old at the time. We had found an old leather trunk up in the attic, where we should not have been. But it was raining hard outside.

In the trunk was a whole heap of old papers which we presumed were Grandfather's because the trunk smelt just like him.

Quite silently, mother had appeared behind us, to find out why we had gone so quiet. She looked into the trunk. It must have meant a lot to her, but we of course were oblivious to that. She stretched her hand into the pile of junk and drew out a photograph album. Brown leather like the trunk. She sat on the floor, much to us boys' amazement because mother never ever sat anywhere; she was always too busy to sit. As she opened the pages she turned into a little girl.

'Look! That's me! I must have been about your age. Look! There's Jimmie! That's our dog. Our wire-haired fox terrier. James. He was a true gentleman. He was my friend. My best friend.'

She showed us the picture. It was a large family group photo such as was so much loved by families in the early nineteen-hundreds, posed carefully for the man from the photographic studio who will just have said 'Now everybody, keep quite still for me please … Quite still.' The picture was full of people. All ages. All sorts. Mother's parents we supposed (was that really Grandad?), and her mother (who we never knew), and her brothers and sisters (six of those), and the governess and the nanny (considered – unlike the kitchen, stable and garden staff – to be part of the family), and some others, which must have been uncles and aunts. But no dog.

'Where's the dog, Mum?'

'There!'

She prodded at the fading sepia picture. There, beneath her long white skirt was the moustachioed face of a scruffy terrier. Peering out, folded-over ears set high, guarding his mistress.

'That's Jimmie! He was a good dog.'

By that, Mother did not mean he was a well-behaved dog. Mother did not count good behaviour as adding up to much. By all accounts she had been a wild child. Good behaviour was never really of much interest to her. What she meant was that James was good at being a dog.

It must have struck us at the time, because we responded to her with, 'Who's this? Who's that old woman in the wicker chair with wheels? Who's that one – are they your brothers?' Because she had not noticed any of them, nor thought them worthy of pointing out to her children. All she had noticed in her grand family photograph was her dog. Of all the lot of them, there were only two people in that picture: the girl, and the dog.

Mother rarely referred to dogs as a species. They were lurchers, alsatians, Reverend Jack Russells, deer hounds, Welsh collies, Pembroke corgis, and so on. Just like she never referred to cows. Always Shorthorns, Devon Reds, those horrid Friesians. It wasn't that she made any effort in this regard, it was just that in her mind the word 'dog' could not describe a *being*. All God's creatures were to be properly respected. And all dogs were especially worthy of respect – even the foxhound puppies gulping down half-rotted pig carcasses.

All her own dogs were named within the day of getting them. This was not solely to allow proper recognition. It was that only after being *named* could an animal go to heaven. That was important to Mother. She could not imagine heaven as being without animals. She would be looking forward to meeting all her dogs in heaven, where they would be waiting for her. She never gave a thought to meeting people there, it was her dogs that she wanted to be with again, and they would be waiting, to welcome her home.

*****

Mother rode to hounds from the day she could ride, which was probably when she was six or seven. She hunted with the South Devon pack of foxhounds, which was the private property of one of her uncles. The family owned most of the Devon South Hams as well; the hunting extending out onto the open reaches of Dartmoor.

She was completely familiar with a hunting pack, the whole panoply of their skills coming as second nature as much to her as to the dogs themselves. She knew how they would draw (quarter) a covert, how the fox once flushed, would break. Having put up a good running fox she knew how the pack would work as a team to maintain the scent trail and hunt their quarry down, yodelling to each other in full voice.

Hence the wire-haired fox terrier, I suppose. Jimmie would have been put to good use if Mother had anything to do with it. She was nothing if not utilitarian.

I had not realised it before, but I had misinterpreted Mother's love of horses. The love was in watching the hounds work, and for that matter watching the fox outfox the pack. Her horse was a means to an end. For Mdother, that end was her love of dogs.

$$*****$$

Mother had picked up Jimmie from a basket of puppies she had come across in Capel Curig on the way back from a family picnic in Snowdonia; she must have been twelve or thirteen at the time. Her father and mother were not best pleased to have suddenly acquired another family member (having six children and a substantial retinue of maids and servants already).

The family had moved up to the Wirral to be nearer Liverpool where her father had a job at the University. Previously, he had taught the Cadets of Dartmouth Naval College how to blow things up. Down in Devon, Mother's grandmother ruled over a miscellany of badly behaved children and grandchildren, the whole family sharing a huge mansion outside Paignton.

It was the girl in the family that my grandfather stole.

One of Mother's uncles had the stables and a pack of foxhounds as well as a sizeable chunk of Devon's farming land and moor around the river Dart. Another won for himself the Military Cross and an early death in 1917. The eldest lived the life of a gentleman of means, with socialist intentions. The fourth uncle had a fetish for the colour blue, but perhaps more importantly he was a misogynistic misandrist recluse with an insatiable desire to collect things – books, coins, plants, animals. So many animals in fact, that he needed to found a zoological garden! He also filled the big house with animals both tame and wild, including a plethora of dogs.

Mother's Uncle Giles was obsessed with selective breeding to achieve 'improvements' of one sort or another. He bred cattle, heavy horses, birds, pigs, but especially dogs – starting with his brother's foxhounds. One such improvement would, of course, entail the colour blue. Everything was bred with a view to it bearing offspring that carried genes for blueness in their skin or coat.

It was in the company of her Uncle Giles at the big house that my Mother developed her childhood love of animals – especially the dogs. She lived more often with her uncle, her grandmother and the animals than in her own family house in Dartmouth!

While she was there at her grandmother's house she watched in awe as her Uncle set about breeding one champion dog after another. The first Best-in-Show at Crufts was one of her Uncle Giles' greyhounds – *Primley Sceptre*. He also bred winning gun-dogs (setters and spaniels), and whippets. He was not interested in pets, only dogs that were useful. Mother's heart was first with the foxhounds and next with the (blue) great danes. She liked her dogs big!

Mother was bereft when the family had upped sticks to leave their rural Devonian idyll in exchange for a townhouse without any animals of any sort. She must have been miserable in the environs of Liverpool, miserable enough to lift from its basket that puppy she would name Jimmy.

Mother never lost those roots: foxhounds, working dogs, big dogs.

*****

My own following of hounds started much as had Mother's, though my early memories of the local foxhound pack were neither of the horses nor the dogs. Well, if it was horses, it was because they were either dead or about to die.

Tradition has it that every horse loves to follow a pack of hounds in full cry, which is certainly true. If that is their passion, then they will be wanting to continue to be with the pack in their next life (all horses have proper names, do they not? And they will therefore go to heaven, will they not?). How are we to help?

Obviously, by feeding the dead horses to the foxhounds! In truth, though dead hunt horses did indeed comprise a good part of the foxhound's diet, it was nothing like enough. So, in addition to some oat meals, the pack would get to eat cow, sheep and sometimes pig. It was a most environmentally friendly way of dealing with the farm's regular outgoing flow of cadavers!

My own early memories therefore were not so much of dogs, nor of horses, but of the hunt kennel-man who came to pick up from our farmyard the dead, and – if he arrived soon enough to dispatch them – the dying. It is no surprise that the coming of the kennel-man into our farmyard was a most impressive event to be witnessed by any seven or eight year-old country boy.

Jackman was a person to be reckoned with.

Never *Mr* Jackman. The hunt servants, the paid kennel-men, the paid huntsman, and the paid whipper-in were always referred to only by their surname. (The hunt staff were all paid weekly in coinage. Terms of employment were: holidays (if any) at discretion of the Master; negotiation of wage, none; notice of dismissal, none; explanation of reason for termination of employment, none.) The old retainers if they were senior enough – like the huntsman – could occasionally be referred to by the Christian name they were baptised with, but only in this event by the equally senior and aged members of the County establishment. The hunt servants themselves would have been offended to have been addressed by any other than their family name.

Jackman it was then who would clatter and clank into our farmyard to pick up the next day's breakfast for his hounds, the ancient horsebox coughing and wheezing its way to a creaky halt in the middle of the cobbles. Getting down from the driver's seat was a slow and painful event for Jackman because, to the considerable fascination of us boys, he had a wooden leg. This meant that he walked with his right leg describing an arc as it swung round in asymmetric rhythm to propel Jackman forward, lurch by lurch.

Once alighted, the figure of Jackman would be a thing of wonderment, for he was obviously a cowboy from the American Wild West! Straight out of the comics that had come to us from the US with the war rations. He wore leather chaps for trousers, and round his middle was slung a wide leather belt upon which hung an imposing holster. In the holster resided a most impressive pistol. To load this weapon, Jackman had a pocketful of bullets.

He would delight in taking the pistol from its holster, holding it by the barrel, then tapping his lower leg with the gun's wooden hand-grip. We would hear the clunk of wood on wood. We boys would scamper about with glee,

'Shew us yer leg, shew us yer leg!'

The wood ended at its top in a half-cup with leather straps and buckles, the whole arrangement starting below his knee and ending with the block that did for a foot sufficient to allow a boot to be laced upon it.

We thought, given Jackman's apparent age, that he had had his leg shot off in some heroic over-the-top offensive in the

First World War. It wasn't so. What actually happened was that he fell into the boiling cauldron that cooked the hounds' dinner.

All the fruits of Jackman's foraging for flesh around the local farms on behalf of his beloved hounds had to be properly cooked on their arrival back at the kennels.

Given the nature of the stuff going into the cauldron it was unsurprising that around and about became an unsavoury, slippery mess. And Jackman slipped. Luckily, he did not go in head first. The foot and lower leg however were beyond saving, so the surgeon sawed it off. The story goes that Jackman took it home with him and, like all flesh, threw it into the cauldron, recycling his leg to his hounds.

My brother and I would follow Jackman at a respectful distance, directing him to the unfortunate animal about to receive the attention of one bullet from his pistol. He was good at his job, for which I'm sure the recipients of his expertise were duly grateful. Not least because if it was one of ours, Mother would have named it. So that was alright then.

*****

Mother must have given up her horses, her hounds and her fox hunting when she went farming with Dad a few years before the outbreak of World War Two. She must have come down a big bump from her previous privileged lifestyle. She got her wish to be a farmer's wife and to spend her life looking after her beloved animals, but she got that wish at the wrong time and fell in love with the wrong man. Our Dad was a casualty of the Depression. He had lost all his money working on the Liverpool stock exchange brokering cotton. She did not get back to her hounds until I myself started hunting.

As a farmer's son, I got to ride to hounds free of charge. Before we set off from the meet to draw the first covert, I had always to ask the Master's permission.

'Permission to hunt, Sir?'

'Of course, dear boy, carry on!'

With me out with the pack, Mother had the excuse to come out too – on foot – and once again follow the hunt, there to see again her beloved hounds at work. And to lend a hand to the Whipper-in when called upon (which was often)! The most frequent exchange I had with the Hunt servants was, 'Er, do you know where your mother is?'

In the meantime, being the hapless wife of an impecunious farmer on a wartime dairy farm, she had to make do with the farm dogs for her canine friends. At that time all farms had at least one terrier (to keep the rats down) and one sheepdog (to work the cattle and chase the feral cats).

We usually had at least two of each, one duo being kennelled outside on the farmyard and the other living in the house (well, the kitchen to be exact – they were non too clean). So mother had the companionship of Rap the (gentle) sheepdog and Biscuits the (ferocious) Jack Russell. But as soon as she started following the hunt again, she could not resist the joy of being surrounded by her old love: foxhounds.

Mother said she preferred hunting on foot rather than being up on a horse because she could get closer to the hounds to see them working through the woodland undergrowth sniffing out their quarry. On two legs rather than four she could better hasten to the woodland edge and see the fox break; a russet streak against the fallen winter leaves. The Huntsman in his red Pink coat would be paying as much attention to Mother as to his pack. It would be for her to tell him when the quarry was gone away, and in which direction Charlie Fox was heading.

She was as dependable as any of the hunt servants themselves, who all thought the world of her.

Mother carried on hunting on foot long, long after I had stopped riding to hounds and had moved far north. Her greatest pleasure was in watching the pack stream across open country, heads down on the scent of a fox heading for a covert maybe two miles distant.

It was not uncommon for her to be there at the end of the day when the 'missing hound' count was done. Then she would be away all over the countryside looking for them. She was good at that too, not least because she knew them all rather well, and anyway she was probably the last person to see them go off on a jaunt. When she found them, often in the half-light of evening, they would happily jump into the back of the Land Rover to be taken home to the Kennels.

*****

Mother's familiarity with the hunt ended up in our farm being persuaded to host hound puppies – 'Puppy-walking' it was optimistically called; it was no such thing! Every year a few of the old hounds were 'retired' and youngsters brought in. The hunt kennels were far too busy, far too cramped, to take puppies on board. They needed open spaces and freedom to grow up in. Farms.

We would have three of these unruly beasts every year. They came at eight or so weeks of age and left us when they had become totally unmanageable. The kennels never seemed in any sort of rush to have them back!

They were, in truth, dire.

The hound puppies lived in a shack behind the farm's stables. Hounds have no idea of domestic hygiene so they and their quarters were permanently stinking. We fed them on a cooked porridge made of cereal (same as we gave the farm animals) and dead pig carcasses. If these were just squashed baby pigs laid on by their mothers they went into the cooking pot whole. Bigger ones had to be cut up. In the bothy by the pig pens was a large (very large) boiling pot which sat on a home-made gas ring.

Every morning the beasts were fed and let out. Once weekly, the boy that had been most naughty and deserving of punishment was directed to muck the puppy kennels out. Father would not have it that the farm workers ever be asked to do such a job. It was the most hateful of tasks. The smell is up my nostrils to this day!

During the daylight hours the young hounds would run wild about the place, worrying the hens, chasing the geese, getting under the cows' hooves, disappearing up the fields to hunt for rabbits, eating stuff out of the midden, defecating at random, turning over the rubbish bins and generally getting kicked by the farm workers when they ventured into any of the stock buildings. They were respectful only of the old sheepdog; she would stand no nonsense from them. At dusk they were fed more of the foul porridge, and with the temptation of their bowls put ahead of them inside their hut, they would be shut away for the night – usually. Once back in their quarters, for an hour or so, they would howl.

We none of us much liked the hound puppies. Mother would remind us: 'They are not companionable. They do not share, they do not give. They are pack dogs. They are hunters, seekers out and runners down of their quarry. They are not pets, they are working churls. They are rather stupid beasts.'

The care that Mother gave the hounds was quite different to the love that she lavished on her own dogs. She loved the hounds for their nobility, their four-square set to the body. She loved the foxhound's pack-hunting instinct, which she admired and adored to watch so much.

The point about the foxhounds was that they were so fundamental to the intricate interwoven warp and weft that is the native countryside. The hounds were part of country life, part of countryfolk's sport, they were the ordinary farmworker's (free-of-charge) recreation. Hounds were there also to control the foxes in the absence of the bears and wolves that once did that job. Hounds were part of the balanced ecology that was our environment.

The hounds were important, not just to Mother, but to all of us. All of our family, all of the farmers around, all of the people who lived and worked in the land and knew the countryside. And for that matter, all of the animals that would be predated if the fox population ran amok; not just the laying hens living in outdoor huts, but the hedgehogs, the pasture voles, the curlews, the partridges, the woodcock, the plovers and all the other ground-nesting birds.

*****

In the immediate post-war years (late forties, early fifties), whilst it is true my own major involvement in 'hunting with hounds' was specifically with the Cheshire Forest pack of fox hounds, hunting as a means of countryside pest control and having a whole heap of fun at the same time, was pretty much ubiquitous.

Stag hunting and otter hunting had fallen away in the Thirties and not much picked up post-war except in the south. But our countryside of small fields for grass, kale and corn, scattered through with woodlands and coppices, was also perfect for hares, badgers and, of course, that staple raptor food – bunny rabbits.

Local to our district was a pack of scratch 'Harriers'. This hunted at weekends when a small group of countrymen (and women) would gather for a 'bit of sport'. The Harrier pack was made up assorted dogs whose only entry qualification is that they could follow a scent. The 'Harriers' were frowned upon as being 'a bit rough'. I could not say whether that was referring to the dogs or the people: probably both. The Harriers hunted anything and everything that they came across.

The smart alternative to the Cheshire Forest foxhounds was the Royal Rock Beagles. It was generally accepted that the only member of the canine species more stupid than a foxhound was a beagle. But I'm sure both were equally highly intelligent – at being pack-hounds.

The beagles hunted hares. There were at that time very many hares in the fields and on the upland rough-grazing areas. There were, indeed, so many that they were judged to be a pest requiring controlling. The beagle pack was smaller than the foxhounds, probably about eight couple. Much like the Cheshire Forest, the beagles were in the private ownership of a well-to-do and mildly eccentric local squire. One was permitted to join the chase at his pleasure.

To control the pack, the Master had a couple of amateur helpers 'whipping-in'. All three were smartly dressed in hunting Pink coats, white breeches, bottomed off with thick green socks and stout leather shoes suitable for running about the countryside. The kennel man wore a bowler hat, but the master and the whippers-in had smart gentrified flat caps (not the sort worn by the Liverpool ship workers!). Everybody was on foot, no horses allowed!

The foxhound pack drew coverts, knowing that the foxes, stopped out of returning to their earths with sticks and stones, would be lying up somewhere in the woodland undergrowth.

Beagling was a more random affair, the hounds being set to quarter a large area of likely ground in the hope of putting up a hare. Much, I suppose, as we boys did on the farm with the sheepdogs: open places were known where hares abounded.

Again in contrast, the fox, once flushed from the covert, would make a relatively straight line across country to seek refuge in some spot a distance away, but known to Mr Foxy. This is why following foxhounds was such fun: only the fugitive knew where he was going. The hare, on the other hand, seemed to have no notion of seeking sanctuary at some far off place of safety. The hare's defence was to bolt and dart, to zig and zag, to rush and pause, to go in a large circle, while the beagles tried to make sense of it all. In consequence, those following foxhounds could find themselves far from home at a day's end, whereas those running after the hare had a good chance of turning up not that far from where they had started!

Beagling was really quite a relaxing afternoon in the countryside. Following foxhounds on horseback was entirely different. It was much more exciting to face the dangers of charging across unknown terrain, meeting head-on hedges, ditches, rails and gates that each required to be negotiated in their own way. Preferably with a clean leap at full tilt with – once one's horse was lined up and going for it – eyes tight shut! Nowadays that would be called an 'adrenaline rush'. Then it was just a thrill like no other.

*****

Mother's negative opinions of hounds as house dogs was not helped by the serendipitous arrival of Willow. Father brought Willow home one evening, purportedly as a present for Mother. He had been given Willow by a friend (of sorts) at the local inn.

Willow was a bargain for the cost of a couple of pints because she was pure-bred pedigree (or so it was said). Pedigree basset hound. A big, floppy, white and tan bundle of humungous-pawed dangly-eared squishy-squashy uselessness.

Willow got called Widdle on account of the way she never properly got the idea that under the dining table was not where one was expected to make large puddles. When Widdle widdled, the place was flooded. It might have only been a farmhouse kitchen floor, but we lived there too!

Poor Willow was neither hound nor sofa dog. She was too lazy to hunt. She would sniff about a bit, but never bothered to follow up and chase. Neither was Willow lovable enough to be welcomed to join the family on the sofa. The vet said she probably had had a bad birth and suffered oxygen starvation.

Willow just didn't have a proper place in the world. We boys thought, truth be told, that Willow was a waste of space. Mother insisted on looking after her and giving her love, but even Mother's heart wasn't in it. Anyway she had other things on her mind, like four kids and a dairy farm haemorrhaging money.

It was Father who took the initiative. Willow was, according to him, given away to a Harrier pack in north Wales, used by a rough-shooting syndicate which needed a member who was a bit slow, but had a good enough nose. I hope she was happier than with us! If indeed it was to there that she had actually gone.

*****

It was because of the hound puppies that Mother finally put her foot down and got for herself – at long last – her own dog. Her logic was that if the family could put up with the hound puppies (and with Willow) then they could put up with a small and friendly little house dog; one just for herself. She had not had her own dog since Tuppence, her Sealyham terrier, who was with her when she was married. She deserved one now.

As it happened, the dog that arrived was friendly enough, but it was not very small. Not at all small. Rowan was an Irish wolfhound. She had always wanted one. Tuppence notwithstanding, her ambition was for a proper dog.

'But Mother, it's a *hound*.'

'No dear, wolfhounds are quite different.'

There is no logic in the love of dogs. And Rowan was indeed most certainly different.

*****

Rowan got her name on Platform 3 of Chester Railway Station. It appears there had been an exchange of letters (fountain-penned onto Basildon Bond paper) with someone in Norfolk, and the poor wight was put into a biggish crate and dispatched by rail as 'goods going north-west'. She was in a bad state by the time we got her picked up. Apart from her mental condition – being separated from her family to be cooped up in a crate – she was dehydrated, starving and covered with mange. That was why Mother named her so immediately, for fear that the puppy would be dead before we got her home. How long she had been trundled about the country on trains, goodness only knows. With the help of a hammer and screwdriver the dog was de-crated and emerged into a kinder world. She was all leg and head – and about the size of a foal. By the size of her paws, if she survived she was going to be huge. She did; she was.

By the time she was adult, Rowan weighed nearly eighty kilos, was fully a metre high at the shoulder, and when up on two legs, substantially taller than a man. The Irish wolfhound is the biggest (size-wise) of all the dog breeds, though not as heavy as the great dane (and considerably more laid-back).

Rowan was the gentlest and sweetest natured of all the dogs Mother ever had. If she was shut out in the farmyard on an evening and wanted into the house, Rowan was too polite to bark. So she would simply gaze forlornly through the kitchen window until somebody noticed the huge apparition staring in at them from the gloom.

She would welcome strangers who swung their cars into the farmyard by standing alongside the driver's door and placing her paws on the top of the car roof. Her head was at this point high above the vehicle, so in order to peer into the car and give its driver an appropriate welcome her head would turn nearly upside down to get low enough. This contortion was usefully misinterpreted by those of ill intent who would be warned off by Rowan's attentions. She was the opposite of a good guard dog, but her sheer size made her most excellent at the task!

We boys would take her up the fields in the hope of putting up a fox. Once sighted, she would have it caught within a half-field's length! She was swift as light, and killed in the instant. She was wonderful to watch at full tilt on a mission. Mother loved that dog. My memory of Mother somehow always has Rowan somewhere in it, which is probably right. She filled a huge space wherever she was. In the house, Rowan lived on a blanket laid flat on the cold tiled kitchen floor. From that vantage point her eyes followed Mother's every move.

Rowan had a rough black and grey streaked coat, disorderly hairy everywhere, bushy eyebrows, floppy-down ears and a bearded chin. She looked in fact much like an immense wire-haired dachshund. We all loved her.

Mother was insensible to Rowan's totally unmanageable scale. It was like having a pony around the house. She filled the back of the Land Rover, with the result that family outings often necessitated us kids sitting on the floor!

Rowan was allowed – because she was Mother's dog – to sit on the furniture. 'On' being the operative word. The room that always had a fire going in it – where we ate, played, listened to the radio and kept warm – was stone flagged. Ideal for non-too-clean dogs to lie about the place. In front of the fire was a rug, much loved by said dogs. To left and right were two big chairs, one was Father's and one was Mother's. Father would occupy his quite often, for being on a stone floor he could get to it without taking off his leather working boots. There he would nurse a mug of hot tea – standard fare after mealtimes.

Mother's chair was only sat in by Mother in the evening when she had socks to darn. During the day, Mother's chair was allowed to be occupied by Rowan. She could not, of course, fit *in* it. So she sat *on* it. She would back up and plonk her backside down just like any of the rest of us humans, her front feet forward, propping her upright. This regal position she would maintain for hours at a time.

Rowan was bred once, to have a litter of three, amongst which was Tarn. Tarn was Rowan mark II – though there could never be another Rowan. Tarn, being born on the farm, worked out for herself a much more free-ranging lifestyle than Rowan, who rarely strayed far from the house and farmyard unless accompanied by either Mother or us boys. Tarn was a more independent spirit and would roam the extremities of the farm buildings and the adjacent fields.

The youngest child in our family, Susan, had been somewhat replaced in Mother's affections by Rowan – which understandably, like any teenage girl, she resented. Competition for one person's affection between another human and a dog is quite common, not least amongst marriage partners: 'You care more about that dog than you do about me!' Well it's sometimes true. Best to share the dog's affection then!

The idea was that the jealousy would be assuaged by Tarn being called Sue's dog. To some extent (only some extent!) she was. When she made the decision to go to Canada, to be with her newly qualified veterinary partner who had gone as a Junior into a Toronto town practice, the offer was made that she take Tarn with her.

Had this happened, Mother would have been devastated. Not just to lose her beloved (only) daughter, but her dog as well. There was no agonising decision to be made however. Tarn was a very large farm-raised beast. The little Toronto apartment flat was six floors up!

Tarn would appear, unannounced, in the most unexpected of places. Such manifestations on the part of a small dog are always something of a treat resulting in a welcome, followed by a happy coming together with pats and licks. Tarn, however, was even bigger than Rowan. When she appeared it was always a bit of a shock and one could not help but be taken aback. Tarn, of course, would register this and be apprehensive in her approach, asking, 'Am I OK? Is it fine to come and say hullo? Or should I just stand off a bit, gently wagging my extremely long tail and the end of my extremely large body? – I don't want to cause anybody any anxiety.'

Tarn would roam about helping the sheepdogs (which they wished she wouldn't), or she would be checking up on the frequent visitors driving into our farm's cobbled yard.

When not spending time amusing the residents at the expense of the visitors, Tarn was probably back at the farmhouse waiting to be let in so she could do her regular check on Mother, who could be depended on for an uninhibited welcome.

After Tarn, Mother decided that perhaps a slightly smaller dog should occupy her kitchen floor – after all, she had moved out of the farmhouse and into the farm cottage. She and Father shared dogs after that. Though all the shared dogs knew full well who the mistress was.

The Farm's Terriers

Probably entirely erroneously, our family had a rather specific understanding of what a terrier dog was. It was any small dog that would attack without fear or favour anything that it fancied attacking. Top of this list were the farm rats. After that in no order of preference came: cats, dogs other than our own, gypsies, cars, anybody wearing clean trousers, men in shiny shoes. At the bottom of the list were quarries that fell into the 'not approved' category. These were nonetheless also attacked but more circumspectly: sensible terriers made sure no humans were around to witness such events – or a good kicking would ensue. 'Not approved' included hens, geese, horses, pigs, cows' heels, and children.

As well as a ferocious temperament with a tendency to bite first and ask permission later, our terriers had a number of other features in common. They were all small, short in the leg, muscled like a diminutive weight-lifter, and thick and wiry in the coat – a patchwork mix of white with various shades of brown through to black. The forehead was broad, the nose long, the teeth shining white – extremely sharp and meeting with mitered precision when the top jaw clamped down over the bottom in a lock that would not yield until whatever was in their grasp was dead.

Not one of them known to me was ever trained, or trainable. They busied about the farmyard, came with us (if they were so minded) to hunt whatever it was we boys were terrorising, or just curled up by the fire, in the haystack, or on someone else's bed (human or otherwise), to sleep the day away between meals. Their final common terrier characteristic was that they had an uncanny knack of appearing at the gallop at the sound of any vehicle door being opened, to leap inside and occupy the front seat.

It was to be expected that any country person travelling anywhere would do so in the company of their terrier. Every tradesman, farmer, farmer's wife, farmworker, delivery driver, lorry-man, ploughman, stockworker, poacher, gypsy and villain had a terrier about their person. On account of their uncontrollably unruly behaviour, these dogs rarely were let out of their owner's vehicle. If any stranger thought to approach a van or car with a terrier resident, all hell would break loose with frenetic barking and snarling sufficient to raise the dead. Thefts from vehicles were unknown.

In most other characteristics there was little in common to describe the breed. For it was not a breed. The terrier as a breed was an alien concept, a contradiction in terms. The Welsh sheepdog was a breed. The Irish wolfhound was a breed. The farm terrier was a way of life.

*****

Farm terriers must have begun to be divided into separate types around the time the family farm was losing its grip on me and I saw the attractions of life as a student; a seeker after truth that seems to have kept me in employment (hopefully gainful) for all the years subsequently.

Mother's dog Jimmy, which she had in her teenage years, was a proper breed; a 'fox terrier'. This was bigger than the terriers we employed to actually flush foxes from their earths. The 'fox terrier' cut a handsome figure, proud in stature and long in leg. It would never fit down a fox's earth, and if it did it would have come to a bad end.

Our fox terriers were rougher cut, with shorter legs, killers of rats and much else they might have been, but they did not kill foxes. That was not their job.

The fox terrier's employment was to wriggle down into the fox's lair to bark like crazy if Reynard was at home. The barking was so furious and so intimidating that Mr Fox would choose one of the other exits of his domain to break cover in a rush of red, there to meet the guns of the farmers who had tired of losing their hens to nightly fox slaughter; or to be chased over open ground by a pack of foxhounds.

In my youth, the speciality that later came to be called the 'Parson's Jack Russell' was a sneered-at anachronism. It was what the townies thought a fox terrier was. It was bred as a house dog – a pet. That wasn't what the Reverend Russell had in mind at all. The Reverend whose parish was in Devon, was fox-hunting mad – riding to hounds on a daily basis. It seems he found it tiresome waiting for the 'terrier man' to arrive at wherever it was that the fox had gone to ground. So he decided to breed a terrier that could run along with the pack and so arrive on time at the spot where he was needed. The Reverend Jack Russell therefore selected his terrier for long distance running stamina; longer legs being a part of that. It was rough coated and rough natured.

The Jack Russell terriers we came to know later were smaller, podgier, shorter in the leg. They were more dependable as a 'type' than the common-or-garden farm terriers. They began to replace their predecessors as vehicular companions and as the farmhouse (farmer's wife's) dog. These brown and white smooth-haired puddings of joy kept many of the characteristics of their predecessors, the farmyard terrier. They were snappy, bad tempered, child-biting, with a persistent high-pitched yap to top off their general level of unacceptability. They did however dash about enthusiastically, chase after balls, and cause amusement with their antics. They seemed to be replaced after a decade or so of fashion by a variety of lap-dog breeds such as are now the commonplace unfortunate pets of suburbia.

It has to be admitted that the wife of one of my brothers fell under the spell of the Jack Russell fashion, sporting a pair for a few years (they did best in pairs, occupying themselves, snapping at each other rather than at human nephews and nieces). The love affair did not last.

My other brother's wife blotted her copybook by bringing to the farmhouse a King Charles spaniel. The most unsuitable dog imaginable for a farmyard. It did not join in the terriers' fun and games, would not learn from the sheepdogs anything of the arts of herding cattle and pigs, did not ever grasp what it was in the smells along the hedgerows that got the hounds so excited. It did however get very dirty, which necessitated frequent washing-down before it was allowed to occupy its proper living space – the couch.

The disastrous King Charles was fully redeemed however by its replacement, a little Norfolk terrier who possessed a rough-coated square brown body, drop ears and an excess of both charm and fun. Rosie was the life of the farmyard and the house too. She was dearly loved by my brother's family and when they lost her they were bereft. They never got another dog. The pain of losing Rosie had been too great.

By Rosie's time however, things had greatly altered on the farm. In the sixties and seventies things changed on very many family dairy farms. In fact, the small family dairy farm was well on its way to extinction.

Our farm first lost its dairy herd, and with them its sheepdogs. Then it lost its pigs, and with them the source of squashed little piglets to feed the hound puppies. With the stock gone, the farm lost its farmworkers, and with them the terriers. The final straw was the realisation that what was big enough to support a family with a dairy herd of forty milking cows in the 1950s was nothing like big enough to support any farm enterprise of any viable size. The corn went too, and with that the rats and therefore the cats. There was nothing left for the farm terriers to aggravate.

When my brother moved in to the big farmhouse (with the King Charles), Father and Mother took Timmy, the last remaining farmyard Jack Russell, into the farm cottage with them. He turned into a bad-tempered beast with a special knack of being nasty to everyone and endearing himself to no one, not even Mother. After Father died, Mother tried hard to love the dog. She cared diligently for the beast – it was the last one that the two of them had shared. But she was relieved when Timmy finally left this earth allowing Mother and the farm cottage to rest in some sort of harmony.

After Timmy, there were to be no more 'farmyard terriers'.

Mother lasted only a few weeks without company in her house. An eight-week-old puppy duly arrived on her doorstep, courtesy of neither Father's jacket pocket nor Uncle Bert. Probably from the butcher, who knew Mother well enough to know she would be needing a dog, but would not herself ever have requested one.

Meg, her long-legged, white, wire-haired Jack Russell, outlived her. They had a good dozen happy years together, doting on each other in constant companionship through to the end. We never thought that Mother would love any dog again as much as she had loved her wolfhounds; but little Meggy was the best of the lot. They were inseparable.

Mother knew she would soon die, and was reluctant to do so and leave her dog uncared for. A home was found for Meggy, a family with children. Mother knew them. Content that her little dog would be happy in a new home, Mother let go.

Meggy was, however, never a farmyard dog. It has to be faced that she was one of the new sort of Jack Russell – a pet, not a killer.

*****

Our local hunt never had any of the Reverend Russell's terriers running with the foxhound pack. We had a Terrier Man.

The Terrier Man was a countryman of the old school. He lived in a two-room sandstone cottage which at one time had an oat-straw thatch roof, but now had to make do with rusting corrugated iron sheets. In summer he found work ploughing, making hay, harvesting or threshing. In winter he did hedging and ditching for all the local farms. He knew intimately the countryside and all the beasts and plants that lived in it. Not because he had made an effort to learn any of it; but because he was an integral part of it.

He knew every fox earth in every wood. No hunt could manage without a man to carry the terriers and do the earth-stopping. He was the backbone of the hunt. Every pack of hounds had one of his kind. Today things have changed. There aren't any of them left now.

Our hunt Terrier Man carried his two rough-haired dogs in a big leather bag; much in the same way as he carried his polecat ferrets. These dogs were of no particular breed other than 'farm terrier'. They were expert at flushing foxes; they got plenty of practice, and not just when the hounds were out!

The same Terrier Man was also depended on to do the 'earth-stopping' on the night before the day that the hunt would be meeting. The Meet was either at a pub or at a farm; both needed only to supply ample parking for the horses' boxes and ample rum punch for the horses' riders. For any location, a half dozen or so woods would be drawn. It would be essential that the resident foxes were not tucked up safe in their earths when the hounds were sent into the covert, but lying out amongst the undergrowth.

To achieve this, the Terrier Man would have spent a good part of the previous night stopping up the foxes' earths, spade in one hand, hurricane lamp in the other, dogs in his bag. Short branches, sods, sticks and stones were pushed into the entrances and exits of Reynard's residence. When Foxy would return to his lair in the early hours of the next day, having completed his night of foraging around the countryside and farmyards, he would find his way back into his house barred.

At the end of the hunting day, everybody went home after an exhausting but satisfying time following hounds; jumping hedge, ditch, rail and five-bar gate. The hunt followers would sup their nightcaps and retire content to their (or someone else's!) beds. And all the while, the Terrier Man would be out and about again, with his hurricane lamp to light the night, unstopping all those earths so the fox population too could have a quiet night of rest in their proper beds.

I spent time, day and night, with our hunt Terrier Man. I learnt from him that country craft cannot be taught. It has to soak in – gradually, naturally, generation to generation. He did not make 'observations' about the country ecosystem as do today's environmentalists; he was, body and soul, an inherent part of it. His wisdom is now lost; and the countryside is so much the worse for that.

*****

Paddy M'Ginty arrived, as did all our terriers, fished out of one of Father's jacket pockets on his return one evening from the Boat Inn. He was the first dog that I could call 'mine'. Paddy grew a fine pair of testicles, the contents of which were regularly deposited into the oviducts of every bitch (of any size) on heat for miles around. He was often away from home seeking out another mistress. It never crossed our minds to have any of the dogs castrated (nor for that matter the bitches spayed). We castrated every other male mammal on the farm: the calves, the piglets, the horses, but never the dogs.

Paddy would sleep in my bedroom at night in a wicker chair. He was there in that chair when I was ill, had my tonsils out, was lying flat and useless with polio. He was my chum. We spent the day together, around the farm; we would hunt together amongst the hedgerows, dig at the rabbit burrows, fish for perch in the ponds, find rats in the haystacks. Paddy would be there to help with the chores like feeding the pigs, putting the hound porridge on to boil, grooming the horse. We made a threesome when I went hacking up the fields, and if I was riding along the quiet country lanes, he would come along then too.

This idyllic pattern was broken however by term times at boarding school. I hated school in any event. Though Paddy made my life at the farm infinitely better by his companionship, his absence when I was at school made things infinitely worse there. I needed Paddy at home and he was there for me. I needed Paddy a whole lot more when I was at boarding school and he was not there for me.

Paddy was a farm terrier for two-thirds of the year, and my dog for the remaining third when I was home. Paddy was particularly adept at ratting. He had been bitten on his nose when a youngster and wore the scar for the rest of his life. But he was never bitten again.

In the end, Paddy stayed at the farm for longer than I did. I was not there when he died. I was not told of the circumstances but he had ended up under the wheel of a tractor.

*****

The stable building was on the fourth side of the farmyard, the other three being, respectively: the shippons in which lived the milking cows, the loose boxes for the young stock, and the farmhouse. The barns were separate spaces where lived the ploughs, the turnip chopper, workshop, the hens, the grain and the hay, and the pigs. Entry to the barns was 'round the back'.

The stable, shippons, loose boxes and farmhouse were all entered directly from the farmyard. The yard itself formed an enclosed square (which at one time had a well at its centre) with an entrance gate. This gate would invariably stand welcomely open, unless Foot and Mouth disease was rampaging about the countryside, in which case it was padlocked firmly shut. On one side of the gate ran a fine sandstone wall, the purpose of which was to keep the animals, all except the dogs that is, out of the vegetable patch. In this the wall failed – the chickens, like the sheepdogs, being no respecters of walls!

There was also an exit from the farmyard, through which passed every morning those going to work in the fields and through which returned every evening those weary of the day; wishing only for their supper and (if fortune smiled that night) a warm bed.

Out on the farm's pastures and ploughed lands every field had at least two gates, one of which was usually unserviceable and the other barely serviceable, needing to be lifted before it would open or close because its hinges had dropped.

The gate out of the farmyard however was always in tip-top order, opening and closing on a push and a click, free swinging on an instant. It wasn't just that it had to be because it was by far the most used gate on the farm, but because it was also the one on public view, seen by everyone who came into the yard. As Father said, 'A man can be judged by his boots, and a farm by its gates'.

When it was built in the 1800s, it was fundamental to the working of the farm that the stable was in the prime location; equally accessible from the farmhouse and, through that finely hung gate, the fields. Little surprise then that after the horses were all gone, if you wanted to know on any farm where the dogs might be, it would be the stable.

It was in the stable that the farm terriers and the on-the-loose yard dogs would bunk-up, be fed, whelp, and die. The stable smelt not of horse, but of damp dog. On a farm it helped a lot if you liked that smell of wet unkempt dog.

Because it was dog territory, the stable was also a safe place for us kids. The pigs were not safe, they bit. The cattle squashed and kicked. And for some reason when we came into the farmhouse smelling of pig or cow mother would object; but she never turned a hair if we smelt like the dogs!

The stable had four wide stalls at ground level, with a loft (for hay) above. The stalls were wider than you tend to see nowadays in stately mansion stable blocks renovated into tearooms. Those were for carriage horses – of lighter build than the farm cart horses. Our stalls were for horses rather wider in the beam! I have no idea what sort of horses we had. When we were down to two, they were probably Clydesdales (most were), but only ever referred to as 'the horses', or by their given names. Our last horse was called Flower. By the time we had only Flower left, there were already two tractors – Fordsons (one green, one blue), cranked up by a handle with a kick more wicked than any horse.

As a mixed Cheshire dairy farm, we were originally, as evidenced by the stable, a four-horse farm. The number of horses that a farm would need depended on its acreage of tillage and the 'heaviness' of the soil. Our place was not large, but the land was all heavy, muddy, boulder-clay. By the 1950s Flower stood alone as the sole equine occupant of the stable. The other three stalls were dog and children territory. Flower was used to dogs and children mucking about the place and getting under his huge feet – given his last-survivor status, he probably enjoyed the company.

Flower was kept on because in winter his four hooves could pull a cart loaded with turnips where no wheeled tractor could even pull itself. Three days a week through the winter months, Flower would be tackled up by the Tractorman (previously the Horseman), put between the shafts and off up to the turnip field with us two boys reluctantly making up the snagging gang.

We would invariably be joined by the terriers, who would share with us the floor of the cart (going up), or the top of the turnip load (coming back). Pulling, snagging, loading and carting the turnips was horrible in the cold wet winter days, only made bearable by the terriers' perpetual fooling around along the hedgerows and in the ditches looking for water rats, hedgehogs, or the occasional buck-rabbit lying out.

While we were working those horrid wet cattle turnips, the terriers would busy back and forth around the cart. There was never any danger of their being trodden on. Flower never trod on a dog in his life, but there was always a threat from the cart wheels.

The obvious solution of throwing the dogs up into the cart would be destined to fail as they would be bombarded by the turnips being flung in after them. The only safe place was up on top of the horse. Or, to be precise, on top of the horse's broad backside. Generously wide in all directions there was ample room for a terrier or two up on top of Flower's backside. Flower minded not one whit; even when the dogs decided to take exception to a flock of birds, or whatever, and kick up a cacophony of agitated barking.

Paddy, the fiercest of the terriers, was so taken with the elevated position afforded by Flower's kind patience and ample bum that he would ask to be put up every time Flower was harnessed for work. There Paddy would sit, for an hour at a time, swaying gently from side to side as Flower went about his work with steady measured pace. It is unremarkable, in retrospect, to find that when the farms lost their farm horses, the terriers took to riding in the tractor cabs.

Tractors however were never as careful where their feet went as was Flower and his ilk. Dogs being damaged by farm equipment seemed rare in the horse era. But it became a constant threat when every busy farmyard came to be characterised not by the considered clop of a hoof, but by the impatient roar of an unseeing, unfeeling combustion engine.

It was a tractor wheel that ended Paddy's life. Flower would never have been so careless.

*****

All the farm terriers came into their own at threshing time.

Through late summer and autumn the sheaves of cut corn were carted down to the farm where they were carefully layered into large stacks the height of three-storey houses. Our farm would have about four of these. The stacks would sit for a month or two awaiting the threshing gang.

Threshing was winter work. Into the yard, alongside the stacks would roll a huge steam tractor. Powered by coal it would chug along towing behind an even bigger Ransomes Threshing Box. This was an elephant of a thing, a huge pink affair, looking much like a big wooden shed save for the wheels and pulleys gracing both its flanks; these joined together by chains and thick webbing belts. The threshing tackle was completed with a straw baler.

When set up, the tractor would have its huge fly wheel attached with an immense belt in a figure-of-eight up to the much smaller wheel on the threshing box which turned the drum at high speed to knock the grain from the ears. The same wheel would feed on to all the other working parts; the straw walkers, the chaff winnower, the grain shuttles. A final belt, longer than the others, looped back, going from the box on to the baler, powering the cast-iron ram that pummelled the straw tight into an orderly wire-bound bale, the shape of a huge brick.

The whole thing was a cacophony of clanking, banging, whirring, spinning; all set within a haze of escaping steam and smoke from the engine's boiler fire. The tractor rocked backwards and forwards as it chugged away, the box howling at such a volume that it could be heard all around the parish. The baler meantime would be thumping out its inexorable rhythm.

We boys just loved it! But what we loved best of all about threshing was the rats. The bottom layer of every stack would be sniving with rats.

The threshing tackle came with a team. The tractor man, the baler man, the loader man and the team boss. To this would be added all our own men and any others who could be mustered for the week. In total there would be thirteen or fourteen. Mother had to feed and water the lot. It was an immense task; a huge occasion, much bigger than the gathering of the harvest itself.

It was also extremely dangerous. Accidents were commonplace – many horrific. There were no guards on any of the wheels or belts. The loader man who fed the sheaves down directly into the spinning threshing drum stood inches away from being cut to ribbons. To get from one side of the tackle to the other, you had to duck down under the lashing belts.

The key jobs were done by the team that came with the outfit. The rest were done by the farm labourers and the family: bagging the grain and weighing it off into 140lb (64kg) hessian sacks; carting to the granary; heaping up the weed-seed and the chaff; feeding the wires through the straw baler; stacking away the new bales.

On top of the big stacks, two men threw down to the loader man perched on top of the threshing box which was positioned alongside the stack. The job of sheaf-throwing required care and precision. Each sheaf had to land exactly at the feet of the loader. He was stood on a small platform with no room for manoeuvre. He got cross if he had to stretch; he got into a fury if he was hit by a badly placed sheaf. He was in constant fear of his life.

As the main stack went down layer by layer, the throw-down of the sheaves would become a throw-across, then a throw-up with a two-pronged pitching fork.

When two layers only were left at the bottom of the stack, work was halted.

Mugs of tea were dispensed. Thick sandwiches of Cheshire cheese and strawberry jam. All was quiet as the baler belt was decoupled and the tractor flywheel disengaged. Only the gentle chuff-chuff of the tractor remained. All was still, the air full of eager anticipation. The fun was all set to begin.

Now, as will have been gathered, there was amongst all those men a goodly number of their constant companions – those tan and white terriers. Added to the visitor numbers were the home team – the farm's own terriers. And for good measure the dogs from in the farmhouse. A threshing day could well muster a dozen terriers.

They could all smell the rats! They could see the rats! The sheaves were moving with them, the place literally heaving with their slinky dark-brown, scaly-tailed, whiskered-snouty bodies.

Having worked their way down the stack into the bottom layer of sheaves there would be scores of well-fed rats. Big bucks, fat dams, quick-witted youngsters.

All with nowhere now to go.

Most of the terriers brought by the threshing gang were tied round the neck with bits of rope, tethered to any convenient bar or ring. The farm's terriers were confined to the stable. Now the moment had come for the terriers to be let loose. Mayhem! A bedlam of shouting men, frantic barking dogs, squealing rats. The men venturing onto the remaining layers of sheaves were ready to spear the rats with their pitch-forks – trousers tied at the ankle with binder-twine bowyangs so the rats could not run up their legs. The terriers would go wild equally in fury as in delight. A big buck rat is no mean challenge for a dog – even a farm terrier. In the stack bottom the dogs were up to their pink tummies in biting rats; both hunter and quarry fighting for their lives.

The terrier technique is to grab the rat by the shoulder, close the jaw into a lock, and *shake*. Shake like mad. Shake like your life depended on it. The terrier shake is so violently fast that the rat is just a blur. Being thus shaken from side to side, the rat cannot get a bite in – even though his head may be free. It is just being shaken too fast.

Shaken to death.

Sometimes a less experienced terrier will throw the rat into the air. This is not best practice. A thrown rat may go anywhere, and whatever it next meets will be the recipient of a nasty bite.

Good sport for man and dog though the rat-fest at the bottom of every stack was, for us boys it was also fraught with danger; from being stuck with a pikel, bitten in various parts of the anatomy, or tripping in the general fracas to land face-first into a dead rat or a live terrier, which in ratting mood will (like the rat) bite anything moving within reach.

In due course, the chaos would abate as the last of the rats were gleefully dispatched.

With some semblance of quiet restored, the dead rats were collected into hessian sacks and the terriers rewarded with remnants of cheese sandwich kept back for the very purpose.

The clever rats that had escaped the wipe-out invariably made the less than clever decision to seek refuge in the bottom of the next adjacent corn stack!

*****

Sam appeared, just like all the others, out of Father's jacket pocket one evening about half-past-ten. In Sam's case however it was a job to find him. He was tiny. He must have been six weeks old, but still could be fully enclosed in the fist of one hand. He was given to Brenda. Brenda lived with us as part of the family for as long as I could remember; she had come early in the war years to help out and stayed. She was like an aunt to me, a Fairy Godmother in a way.

I don't imagine Brenda asked for a dog. She was never over-fond of the other farm terriers, tolerated the hound puppies with a bad grace, and saw the sheepdogs only as low quality farm-hands. Mind, compared to her own quality of work, nobody could aspire to Brenda's high standards.

Except Sam.

Sam grew to be the smallest, most courageous little dog. He was half the size of any of the other farm terriers, but they were all terrified of him. His stature was that of a terrier in miniature: half-dropped ears, square body powered by sturdy legs, black and tan wire coat, a convincing armoury of teeth, a broad face.

Sam loved Brenda (it was reciprocated) and hated everybody and everything else. Even though the smallest, he was the champion ratter amongst champions. He never missed! He also attacked the farmyard brush with an intensity of hatred that would frighten the life out of any broom. He bit at the pigs and us boys with impunity. We teased him, which really wasn't fair, but we both got bitten by Sam. Mother was not sympathetic. The dog had Mother (as well as Brenda) on his side! Any other dog biting a child was in danger of being dispatched by Father with his .22 pistol. Two bites and you're out! But not little Sam.

He spent his days happy about the farmyard, usually within sight or sound of wherever Brenda was, unless he was ratting. He was the best-ever ratter. Sam spent his nights by the fire as a family member, having elbowed all the other dogs aside.

He was just another farm dog, but as it turned out, the one with the most lasting legacy of them all.

After Sam, Brenda was never without a little dog at her side until she went into the old people's home. She went on to have a succession of Sam lookalikes (only not quite so diminutive). One of these, a prick-eared Norwich which she called Samatha, went on to have a puppy that would be the first dog to grace Chris and my lives together. Our first dog! We called her Brandy. Like the previous generation however, all our dogs were, of course, never mine. They were always Chris's.

Mother's dogs.

Farm Dog: Urban Dog

The farm dogs followed the seasons of the farming year just as we all did.

We had to. The farm ran by its seasons.

True, the pigs lived mostly indoors and their food came in a bucket, while the dairy cows were milked twice a day whatever the day, whatever the weather.

But even the dairy cows knew that spring came with the big release from the neck-chains in their stalls – the mad gallop from the yard, up the lane, and out into the wide fields of fresh grass to graze. It was to the amazement and fury of the sheepdogs, to see the cattle allowed to behave so badly, and to see we humans not only seeming to encourage the cows to leap and buck with uncontrolled joy, but to join in with them, whooping and yelling at the antics of forty staid old ladies kicking their feet in the air, gaily abandoning all pretence at decorum; tits flying left, right, and indeed upwards.

Of course, within the hour, normality would be resumed, the cows' heads soon going down to gorge on the new, sweet young grass. The dogs would only have a few hours to wait before their turn would come; off they would be sent to boss the cows once more and chivvy them back down for afternoon milking.

The hard graft of spring work on the fields – the ploughing, the sowing, the harrowing – was not shared by either sheepdog or terrier. For them it was an excuse to follow the workers up the fields and spend the day hunting the hedgerows and digging in burrows, sport only broken by lunchtime sharing cheese and jam sandwiches, taken seated on the ground under the nearest convenient oak.

Same routine as for harvest time. Just another reason for a jolly if you were a farm dog. Though there was added drama if it was discovered that there were rabbits hiding in the standing corn. As the binder cutter-bar toiled round the field in ever-decreasing circles, the rabbits would get corralled up in ever-reducing space, until finally, they had to make a bolt for it, out of cover and across the open stubble. Few if any made the sanctuary of the field hedges. Swift and nimble though they were, rabbits were no match for the sheepdogs – or the wolfhounds. As for the terriers, they just rushed around barking furiously with glee at the general goings on.

The rabbits, having been nobbled by the dogs, were separated from canine jaws with some difficulty by us boys, to be promptly skinned and gutted. Both pelt and intestines were unceremoniously slung into the hedge for the benefit of that night's gathering of raptors and scavengers. The carcasses themselves were laid out on the (usually rather unsavoury) outside layer of a farm-worker's jacket, with another laid on top to keep (not wholly successfully) the blue-bottle masses at bay. Those who had worked the day in the field would be pleased enough to take the rabbit-meat home for the stewing pot, a free supper for the following evening. Being the 'proprietrix', our farmhouse kitchen got the pick of the rabbit takings – we feasted off rabbit at corn cutting time.

However, even we hungry farm youths would begin to jib at rabbit stew for night after consecutive night. The dogs got much of the left-over rabbit in their own dinners; not much minding the crunch of mixed-in bone.

But even with the dogs to feed, in good years there would still be burgundy-red rabbit carcasses going begging. We would cart our trophies around the neighbourhood, making out that they had been hard won thanks only to our own exceptional skills. The local residents would purchase the bounty for sixpence each, good pocket money for us. However, not all of our neighbours were steeped in the traditions of rural culinary 'make-do-with-what-the-good-Lord-provides'. I imagine after happily relinquishing a sixpence to make the smell go away, the rabbit was consigned to the trash bin.

*****

Strangely, the season of the year that hit our farm hardest was neither seedtime nor harvest; probably because these were spread out over time – much more so than is the case today. Spring work lasted six to eight weeks; same or longer for the harvest if the binder and stooks of sheaves were involved.

No, our biggest challenge came at Christmas. Because of the unremitting intensity of its activity.

Our family dairy farm shared with most others the unfailing ability to lose money. The point of the small family farm was not, of course, profit. It was survival. So although the books (so beloved by the bank manager) showed a steady year-on-year loss, against that loss had to be factored the farmhouse expenditures (otherwise known as family living costs); the mortgage (never paid, the farmhouse was a farm building); all the power costs – fuel, coal, electricity – (never paid, ditto); much of the cost of the food (the farm kitchen fed the workers, so was a business cost); not to count the eggs, milk, chicken and pork etc etc which were simply scavenged, subsistence-style, from the farm itself. Even our hobbies: the shooting, the fishing, all the costs of the horses that used the land and the loose boxes, came for nothing.

At the end of the year the question never was 'Has a profit been made?', but 'Have we survived without too great a loss?' To survive at the end of a zero-sum game was profit indeed!

But what if things were desired that could not be 'acquired' through the farm? A trip to the theatre; fish for a Friday; a holiday week in a caravan at the coast; clothes for school and leisure? These sorts of things needed real money. Money from farm profits.

There was a constant, futile, hunt for ventures that would make real money. We tried rabbit farming – they died of coccidiosis; we tried renting out space to the hunt horses – they ripped the pastures to ruin; we tried a caravan park – the punters got stuck in the thick clay mud and had to be pulled out with the tractor; we tried rearing calves for other farmers – they succumbed to E-coli and pneumonia; the guineafowl rearing enterprise went quite well until they escaped from their pen and sought refuge in the trees; we even tried breeding puppies – but they had to be given away (as was ever so).

Until, that is, when the immediate post-war years yielded a small dividend from those 'Damn Yanks' making themselves at home (sometimes all too much at home) on our shores. With the Yanks came the crazy idea that at Christmas it was a rather sophisticated thing to do to eat turkey.

Father came home from the Boat Inn one spring evening, not with a puppy in his pocket, but with six round brown speckled eggs, a little bigger than double-yolker hens' eggs. These, he explained, would make for us a fortune. Real profit. This we had heard before, many times, but never was any one of Father's grand ideas brought to successful conclusion. On this occasion however, he was nearer the mark than he ever had been, or ever would be again.

Selling turkeys for Christmas roasts to the upper middle-class households of Cheshire's Wirral peninsula was an easy winner. The cost of rearing a Christmas turkey was about half of what it could be sold for, sold to eager customers straight from the farm door.

The eggs were hatched under a somewhat over-challenged bantam hen, who duly taught six healthy young turkeys how to live on the farmyard, how to drive away dogs in a flurry of wings and a clatter of angry squawking. The dogs hated the turkeys with a passion. Not just because they turned vicious as they got older, made a huge amount of silly gobbling noises, and had sharp beaks, but while the dogs were encouraged to chase the cats, round up the pigs, charge at pigeons and indiscriminately kill most other things that moved, if they ever went near the turkeys they were sworn at. The dogs vowed their time would come and they would get their own back, which proved correct.

Wonderfully, the eggs hatched to five hen chicks and one stag. The stag grew big, bold and belligerent. He shared meals with the old boar, the two of them eating out of opposite sides of the old pig's food trough, an arrangement which lasted until the pig lost patience with the fowl and bit the head right off of bold John Turk. The headless body fell flapping on the passage outside the pig pen. His head fell inside, into the trough, convenient for it to be chomped up by the pig in two satisfying gulps.

John Turk had, fortunately, got around all the girls (his sisters) before his demise. His offspring were hatched under their mothers. Summer of that next year found some thirty turkeys on the farm, destined to be fattened, killed, plucked, dressed and trussed ready to be picked up by happy punters on Christmas Eve. It was the first time I got to unfold one of those huge white five-pound notes.

How to kill a chicken by violent dislocation of its neck from its head is early learned on a farm. It is simple. But a hen would be less than a fifth the weight of a turkey bird. Added to that, the bigger bird was more vigorous, more sinewy, more aggressive than any passive layer chicken. The turkeys would put up a fight. This the dogs greatly enjoyed. Seeing off a turkey ready for warm plucking was always cause for a dog gathering; a semi-circle of gloating spectators revelling in the last wing-flapping death throes of the hated turkeys.

The turkey 'business' was so lucrative that it was decided (by Father, needless to say) to have a hundred the next year. Not hatched from eggs under birds, but 'bought-in' as young turkey chicks. Father's mathematics was never strong; he hugely under-estimated the difference between the Tractorman, the Dairyman, and the GFW together with us boys and Mother, setting to and converting – in the twelve days before Christmas – thirty-odd gobbling birds into festive fare, and the same labour force doing the same job in the same time for more than three times as many birds.

It nearly did for us all.

Daytime was for killing and plucking, evening for spending pulling out intestines (properly termed 'dressing', though it was more the opposite), nights were for trussing and packing. Next morning, before the allocated batch of gobblers was dispatched from the land of the living, there were, of course, cows to be milked, pigs to feed.

And, given that the first birds would be ready for sale up to ten days before Christmas Eve, there was a lot of praying to be done too – for cold weather! Being an ordinary farm there was no cold room, only a loose-box in which the birds could be hung from the roof beams.

There was by-product from these efforts by way of damaged birds, unwanted offal, and so on. Needless to say the beneficiaries were the dogs. The big gas ring in the piggery – usually employed in cooking piglets carelessly squashed by their mothers – was readily adapted to turkey cookery. The addition of rolled-oat pig mash to the boiling broth making a fine rich porridge, the envy of any dog within smelling range (probably well more than a mile in dog sniff), eliciting unwelcome visits to our turkey operations by many and various sheepdogs, mongrels, terriers (and even the odd hound) from the neighbourhood.

The profits from the enlarged 'Turkey Job' were, if anything, greater per bird than before, benefitting from 'economies of scale'. Needless to say, as the 'Turkey Job' was the only enterprise keeping the farm afloat, it was scaled up year upon year until the inevitable happened. Hundreds of birds strung up in the farm buildings, combined with December weather so mild it did credit to global warming.

We were exhausted, the turkeys festered, money was lost, Christmas was cancelled. That was the end of the 'Turkey Job'.

The dogs were bereft. The farm would last only a few more years before bankruptcy loomed. The dogs were not so much disappointed as redundant as, like the farm that went with them, there was just no place left to call home.

In the 1970s our family lost our family farm. As a teenager, I had walked away from it, having reached the age of sufficient reason to see farming as nothing more than a hard life for poor reward. The farm dogs too lost their farm. But in their case, the farm had walked away from them.

Those places where, 75 years ago, Britain kept its dogs, have mostly gone now. Dogs are no longer farm dogs, country dogs, working dogs; they are urban dogs, house dogs, pet dogs. For our own family dogs, this has meant revolutionary change. No more will 'our dogs' be the farm's sheepdogs, hounds, terriers. Now they needed to be cut from urban cloth.

The environment in which my family would come to expect the family dog to co-exist would be all those places that are *not* farms; the town, the suburbs, the village.

It is not just us and our dogs. The human population of Britain has made the dramatic transition from farm to town in a mere three generations. Nine out of ten of the families employed on the land a hundred years ago are no longer employed on the land. We have taken our dogs with us, presuming that they are as adaptable as we.

In the middle years of the last century I, like most of my generation, set about crossing that divide which separates the farming life from all other sorts.

I did not want to spend my life keeping pigs.

I decided to make myself voluntarily redundant from the farm staff and seek alternative employment. The *dogs* had redundancy forced upon them. The farms that needed working dogs have all-but disappeared.

Very few of today's dogs are finding a proper day's work in a proper dog's job. Those lucky few that *do*, are the Welsh and Border collies on the ever-scarcer sheep farms, the labradors and spaniels still employed to support the shooting fraternity, and the ever-dwindling members of hunting hound packs. The unlucky majority of working dogs – sheepdogs, gun-dogs, hunting-hounds, terriers – are forced unnaturally into the confined servitude of being expected to behave as 'pets'. Many of them prove none too good at it. There is nothing more frustrated than a pet sheepdog with no sheep to work.

Since we set up our own household, Chris and I and our own family have been privileged to have shared our lives with our dogs – lives that would have been barren without them. But I have often wondered if sometimes we have asked too much of an animal whose instinct is to hunt, to chase, to kill, to herd, when we ask them to join us on the sofa or the carpet in front of the fire. When the 'dog-walks' are just that – walks restrained on a lead; rather than the freedom to run free, to investigate, to smell, to trail, to dig, to work.

Maybe there are too many dogs about our urban and semi-urban spaces now. They are there because they are fashionable – adding 'presence' to their owners. Many seem to be not much 'loved and needed'. They have owners who, given the prevalence of professional 'dog-walkers', seem to be often too busy with other more important things than being in the company of those who crave their companionship – their dogs.

I do not remember any of the dogs on our dairy farm not being wanted. If they were not wanted, they were not there! Though we did, I recall, have one (nameless) unwanted arrival. Uncle Bert again I suppose. He was a big collie/alsatian cross. He was good enough with the cattle, but he could suddenly 'turn' and go full-on for people. We had the odd visitor to our farmyard for whom such treatment was quite amusing and probably justly deserved. He was always good value when we boys came across 'poachers' walking casually across our fields with twelve-bore guns over their shoulders. We never had to run the risk of facing up to these characters.

We simply set the dog on them.

Upon which they would dramatically reasses both their position and their purpose.

But this dog, when he took a mind to attack, did not seem to discriminate between the baddies and the good guys. He was the most loyal of dogs. Loyal to what he saw as his immediate family. Everybody else was a threat. Loyal dogs can be dangerous dogs.

He fell foul of Father's 'Two strikes and you're out rule' – dogs drawing human blood twice being summarily put down.

'Grown men might be expected to defend themselves,' Father would say, 'but next time it may be a child by the throat.'

Unwanted dogs in the urban community can with good luck be rescued and rehomed, which is a good thing. Although not without risk.

Since leaving the farm, Chris and I have been defined by our dogs. They have all been wanted, all loved. We have however *not* been invariably successful in providing for them all *they* might have needed from us.

To that extent the lessons of our dogless years, the years between Paddy and Brandy, may have stood us in good stead.

Let me retrace some steps, back to my teenage years.

*****

To everybody's considerable relief, my school and I came to a mutual agreement that it would be better for all concerned if I left at the earliest possible opportunity, which was just prior to my sixteenth birthday.

I hated school. I was so busy being miserable (it was a 'public' boarding school) that I learnt little and did less. Holidays were times that celebrated not being at the dreaded school. I had the farm to run free around, in the company of Paddy McGinty and whichever of the sheepdogs was available. And if it was winter, to be on my horse, following the foxhounds twice a week.

On leaving school, I fell into farm life, there being none other available. A life of feeding calves, removing dung from pig pens, milking cows and wringing the necks of sick hens before they died so Mother could cook them for our dinner. I did however not much like home at that point. Things were not comfortable in the family and living life on a farm needs everybody in the farmhouse to get on really well with each other – or else it becomes a 24-hour a day prison. And one that was cold and damp to boot!

The family doctor it was who came to my rescue. He visited rather regularly, having an unquenchable 'admiration' for my mother.

'If the boy isn't going to stay at school, he should go to a farming college!'

And so I did – one always does what the doctor says, does one not? It was whilst I was away that Paddy met his end. I was dogless, and effectively without family. But the passion with which I hated school carried over to college, except in the opposite direction. I loved it!

So much so that another kind influence in the form of the College Principal instructed me to go to university, which, of course, I had no qualifications to do. But a year at night school sorted that out, and I was away to Newcastle in the far north. University vacations were not spent back home on the farm with the dogs, but rather up north, studying, or doing projects, or joining into other people's research programmes. Besides, a young lady was involved and she lived in Northumberland!

College and early university years were dogless. I was the worse for that, but it hardly registered because I was so busy making a life that was as far distant from the pig pens and the cattle sheds as I could make it. I cared not to notice the absence of dogs.

In later years, it became inconceivable that we could have a family and not have dogs in the house. Apart from that decade, I – we – had family life and dogs written into us. We would see to it that our children would grow up with dogs. Us too. For Chris and I were married when we ourselves were but children.

Being married meant caring about things other than oneself. Caring about each other, about work, about children, about dogs. We had forgotten how dogs could reciprocate that care so readily and generously. But little Brandy would remind us.

Does that suggest being dogless is a state of living less than what it should be? Of course it does. But there are practicalities. Although dogs serve us, they also need looking after: food, exercise, being loved and cherished. There are times in the lives of many modern humans when this cannot happen. To have no dog is better than having a dog forced to live in a place that is alien to the canine soul. Pavements, skyscraper flats, laboratory benches, offices and the like are no places for a dog to live out a dog's life. Sometimes we take dogs into our lives for our own sakes, without asking the dog. Dogs, being dogs, will however accept whatever is thrown at them. And that is at the root of the problem for town dogs.

*****

Fortunately, our own family dogs have been forgiving creatures. Let me tell you all about them…

First Family Dog

Incompatibility between young lovers is invariably shrugged aside on the grounds of those concerned being both young, and busy making love. Incompatibility when that same couple begin to live together in their permanent home can be altogether a more difficult matter. Irresolvable issues can arise: political predilections; toothpaste tube tendencies; driving techniques; dodgy colour co-ordinations; carpet design; … *Dogs*.

I sadly realised soon after marriage that my wife Chris and I were in danger of failing to see eye-to-eye over that most serious of issues. Not over my driving (that would come later), but over the matter of the place of dogs in the family household. Her experiences of 'The Family Dog' had been wholly negative. I came to fear the worst.

When courting, we had spent a few Saturdays following the local beagle pack over the Northumbrian moors. I was forever pointing out the subtleties of the hounds working the rough heather, heads down, following the scent of the hare across field and over wall. It was wasted breath. She was always more concerned for the welfare of the hare; as usual, forever championing the cause of the opposition!

I had not fully realised the importance of this characteristic (I was after all in love with a most attractive girl, therefore doubly blinded), until later when I got her talking about her own dog experiences. But by then it was too late.

Chris' parents by all accounts were not much good with dogs, and dogs were no good at all with them. Which was not surprising in the case of her mother who was brought up in the Chatham townscape. But it *was* surprising in the case of her father who was from the west Durham/Cumberland border country and born on a shooting estate. He was however clearly not much taken with country affairs, becoming one of a small group of well-respected engineers who built and ran the Malayan railway system. After he graduated, he and his wife spent their early lives together in Kuala Lumpur and Penang. The dogs around that part of the world were mostly either for security purposes or were feral; not family pets.

On retirement after the war, Chris's parents came back to the north country to live in a small Northumberland town. They took a fine old stone house on the road out to the woodlands and the moors, complete with a huge walled garden, outbuildings for chickens and so on, together with a generous paddock adequate enough for any pony. Perfect for dogs. They had two in the end, one after the other – Robin and Joe.

That the first dog was slow to appear, and when it did so it was an African breed, a basenji, was the more difficult to understand because just up the road lived Chris's father's two maiden sisters. The Aunties.

The Aunties remained true to their country land-owning childhoods. One of them bred spaniels (cockers and springers), while the other bred white West Highland terriers. You would have thought that the choices there were wide enough ... but a *basenji*? Perhaps the notion of a dog for the children being a good idea had been countered by the idea that a barking dog disturbing the neighbours might be a bad idea. Solution to the impasse? A dog that wouldn't bark – obviously. Hence the arrival of Robin ... Being a basenji, Robin couldn't bark!

Robin seems to have arrived as a youngster, but with a fully formed personality. Possibly a thoughtful gift from the previous owner who had found that as Robin matured from puppy to young dog they had bitten off more than they could chew!

The basenji is a smooth-coated, short-tailed, prick-eared fellow standing about the height of a large Parson's and with similar long legs. It is a hound – bred for hunting. A *hound*? ... bred for *hunting*? Are these ideal qualities in a family pet?

Robin turned out to be an independent soul. He did not stick around the house and the outbuildings the way a Westie might have done, waiting to be taken for a walk or played with by the children. No, Robin was his own man. He took the initiative. He took himself off for his walks. Long ones.

He would go off hunting.

Robin the basenji was well known around the town – and the country.

He went visiting. The shops. The houses. He thieved with great skill. Everybody got to know Robin. Everybody prayed that today Robin would be gracing with his presence elsewhere. There would be telephone calls:

'We've got your dog.' 'We've got Robin here.' 'He seems to like our apples. Our strawberries. Our cauliflowers. Our best pork chops.' 'Can you come and get him?'

For a good number of weeks it was the bluetits who were blamed for taking the cardboard tops off the milk bottles on the village doorsteps, stealing all the cream. Until it was Robin who was caught in the act.

The final straw was, 'Robin's been here. He's been in the kitchen. He's stolen the Sunday roast. We were just getting sat down to dinner. He's eaten the Yorkshire pudding. He's nicked the whole leg of lamb. He's out the door with it.' No sooner was the phone put down than the basenji appeared on his own kitchen doorstep, the incriminating joint clamped firmly between his jaws.

After that Robin was tied up with a lead attached to a ring that ran along a wire. The wire was strung between stakes set out in the pony paddock. There Robin could exercise himself running up and down the length of the wire. It wasn't much of a life for an enterprising dog.

Ever the opportunist, Robin escaped his wire, jumped the field wall and disappeared. He was away three days. It had taken him three days to yank out from the ground the peg that had secured the gin-trap upon which he had trodden. He came home bedraggled, exhausted and with the trap, its chain, and its long peg attached to his front leg. The teeth of the trap's jaws were clamped on his fetlock as firmly as Robin's own jaws would clamp upon a cut of beef.

He had, it seemed, been hunting up in the woods a mile or so north of the house. The gamekeeper there was known to set traps for foxes (they were made illegal in 1958). Miraculously, although Robin's skin and tendons were a frayed, mashed-up mess, the bone itself was not broken. With the attention of the local vet (who was familiar with gin-trap woundings, though the victims were usually nearer death from starvation), Robin was stitched up. He survived to escape another day, but his leg was never the same. He was slower getting underway.

At home, Robin was as nice a boy as you could wish about the house – when he *was* about the house! He was the family dog, good to have around. The family loved him. What was to be done? Robin might now be a bit on the slow side, but he was still the master escapee, the master thief, the master hunter.

In the end, in his inimitable hound way, Robin dealt with the matter himself. Another Houdini escape trick had him through the village and heading down to hunt along the banks of the river Tyne. He was not quick enough crossing the road. He was only four years old.

The tragedy of losing Robin was offset (as such tragedies so often are) by the arrival of a puppy. Joe was a Welsh corgi. My future wife's family were not especially adept at choice of pet house-dog!

Joe had within him all the traits well-known to everyone who has had dealings with Welsh corgis. If they were not disciplined and trained from an early age they would cause chaos within any household unfortunate to have given them house room. While Robin had his endearing characteristics, Joe it seemed, had none.

The Robin experience was by itself enough to have put my wife off dog ownership for good. Like a fool however, I thought that her recounting her memories of Joe might soften her heart. It was a bad judgement call. For it was Joe above all who made Chris completely fail to see what it was about a dog in the house that could possibly bring any sort of pleasure. Joe was a nightmare. It might have helped if he had got more attention, more training, more walks maybe? But he didn't. A King Charles on the couch would have been a much better bet.

Joe began his bad behaviour early in life, his transgressions remaining unchecked. When out of the house he would bark incessantly at anybody deigning to pass along the street, battering at the front gate as he did so. His verbal aggression was no idle threat. Any part of anybody's anatomy attempting access to the front garden or front door was bitten with serious intent. Nobody dared unlatch the gate. Visitors to the house dried up. Excuses were made. Joe made the house a prison for the family by letting no one in.

Welsh corgis were bred as cow dogs. Their small stature made them inherently unsuitable for this task as they frequently got kicked or trodden on by the cows they were meant to herd. The ones to survive to breed in the next generation were the bad-tempered ones that darted in and bit the cows on their legs, down below their hocks. For Joe, any animal with moving legs was something to go for, delivering a full-on bite.

The door bell would send Joe into paroxysms of frantic snarling, so that he had to be put away before the door could be opened. Putting Joe away was itself no mean effort, requiring the combined efforts of two family members. The family itself was not immune from Joe attack. The telephone ringing in the hall would elicit the same response as the door bell. Joe could not stand it. The unfortunate who attempted to go to answer the phone would have their trousers bitten, their heels nipped.

Joe's hatred of nearly everything he found in the world was not restricted to people. He took a dislike to the bantams which as a young girl Chris kept as pets. She took care and attention over her hens and was fond of them. Joe had them in his sights. One special bantam cockerel was disabled, surviving only by the sort of nurture that a child can give. This was Oscar. Oscar had his head twisted to one side, finding pecking grain from off the ground difficult as he had only one eye to focus with. The contortion required to get beak to ground at the exact place that the grain lay was often too much for Oscar – he would wobble about to finally topple onto his side. After which he would dust himself off and start all over again.

Joe had got him. It was hardly a fair fight.

Joe also hated the cat. He kept it well chased, but it had the measure of him, making Joe's demeanour angrier still. Joe's way of getting his own back was to cock his leg and urinate on every surface that the cat had touched. Joe weed on the chairs, the sofa, the carpet, everywhere. He didn't widdle anywhere else except in the house; he kept it stored up to cock his leg wherever it was that the cat had been.

Upon return from school one day, Chris found Joe not there. She knew better than to ask where he was. It was just a blessed relief. Little wonder she wasn't over-fond of dogs.

*****

Chris and I set up our first household in the top floor attic of the house next door to the Aunties. There was room for a bed (a single bed with plywood out-riggers on either side) and two chairs by a single-bar electric fire. The kitchen was a hotplate and basin next to the main house's water cistern. There was no bathroom! The toilet was on the next floor down.

No consideration could be given to any dog. Besides we both had full-time employment, Chris with the MP for Hexham (a bear of a man named Geoffrey Rippon), myself an undergraduate student at the university.

A year later saw us accommodated at the goodwill of the Fourth Viscount Ridley, with whom Rippon's Conservative Agent had had a word about this unfortunate girl married to a poverty-stricken student and living in a garret. It was an isolated gamekeeper's cottage on the Blagdon Estate, positioned on a slight rise in the land above the A1 road north of Newcastle-upon-Tyne. It had a big garden with an unruly shrubbery. There was a back gate that led to the Plessy woods with a path along the river Blyth. The perfect place to have a dog.

Two problems. We were both employed full time (Chris now with the Dean's Office in the Medical Faculty, and me in the Research Lab on the other side of University Road). Second, given her Robin and Joe experiences, Chris was not desperate to have a dog about the place.

Then there was another thing. Young love is blessed with confidence and optimism; young lovers can do anything! I, of course, knew everything about how to look after dogs. I had been surrounded by them all my life.

Except I didn't. I had never looked after any dog! The farm dogs looked after themselves. The house dogs were looked after by Mother – even my own dog Paddy. I never trained a dog. As for Chris, dogs were anathema – but then she had never looked after babies either. Ah! … the optimism of youth.

Brenda, in her own unobtrusive way, stepped once more into my life. She had done so before to engender an appreciation of the arts and music. Then to encourage me into a life with horses. Now she would do it again, by making our family – Chris and my family – a dog family. We would never be without a dog again.

Brandy was one of Samatha's only ever litter of two pups. Brenda gave her to us, we never asked. We just got. That is so often the way with puppies.

Mother had made the long drive to Northumberland from Cheshire to see us in the splendour of our first (albeit grace-and-favour) house, a rare and much-treasured visit.

She had connived with Brenda. On the passenger seat of the (dreadful) Morris Oxford was a small box, snug within which was a tiny Norwich puppy – little Brandy. It remains a mystery why Brenda and Mother wished so strongly that we had Samatha's puppy. They probably just reckoned that now we had a house then we would be needing a dog – naturally! Whatever, we are eternally grateful.

As is also so often the way with puppies, Chris's antipathy toward dogs was transformed the moment she held Brandy in her hands. Brandy wasn't at all like Robin or Joe. Brandy wasn't like Rap, or Paddy either. She was very much her busy, lovable, endearing, forgiving self. She would go on to have much to forgive us for.

Of the three problems, two remained insurmountable. We were both fully employed. We did not have a clue about how to look after a puppy. Fortunately, the third problem – Chris's lack of interest in all things doggy – vanished the moment she had that little puppy in her arms, licking at her face.

The pup would be needing feeding, would it not? The bond was struck. Chris's basic instinct to nurture melded instantly with the dog's basic instinct to be nurtured. There is nothing more satisfying than to see an eight-week-old pup wolfing down its breakfast. Our family twosome had become a threesome; we were a *ménage à trois*.

*****

The gamekeeper's cottage was bare to the boards when we moved in. With no money to spare, we set about furnishing it, which we did for the sum total of £15 10/- spent at an auction house in one of Newcastle's less salubrious neighbourhoods, together with the benefit of a kind donation of a no longer wanted 1950s

Ercol dining-room suite from my university supervisor. A hospital bed was dug up for us by the Aunties out of the back of their garage. This was, naturally, a single bed. We were tight in it, but for a while that was quite satisfactory!

We were now set up in luxury accommodation. More than adequate to provide for a further family member – one very small, square, brown, prick-eared, keen-eyed, dock-tailed Norwich terrier.

Outside, from the wilderness of grass and weeds, a vegetable patch was dug over, I laid the vastly overgrown hawthorn hedge back to manageable height (a farm skill one does not forget), and cleared some at least of the garden scrub. The huge bramble patch gave us a winter's worth of blackberry jam. The shrubbery – a dense thicket of thorn, laurel, hazel and purple rhododendron – was left for another time.

We had a garden that would keep any dog happy. And, when we three were not in the garden, we had only to open the bottom gate to be in the woods and along the banks of the river for as far as we might wish to go.

It was heaven. Our garden remained inhabited by its previous residents: pheasant (Jimmy, who croaked us awake every morning), fox (occupant of the shrubbery and bramble patch), owls (who kept us awake at night), mice, vole, shrew and mole (in the rest of it). Brandy loved it all. There was so much to fuss about, smell and chase. She was a happy little terrier dog – and we were happy dog owners.

It was easy for us to overlook some of the drawbacks of the gamekeeper's cottage. It was cold, extremely cold. In winter our breath froze on the eiderdown at our chins. The bathroom wall accumulated sheets of ice. The only heating was a single fire which had a back-boiler for hot water. That fire had to be kept going 24-hours a day or we were in trouble.

Brandy had her bed in the kitchen. It was a stout cardboard box, closed up on all its six sides, with a little hole cut into it just big enough for her to squeeze through. Within were packed old blankets, we presumed she was snug and warm!

That Brandy's box had a roof proved a godsend when the kitchen ceiling collapsed (following a hole being blown in it when our pressure cooker exploded). The little dog must have been a touch surprised when her sky fell in, but we dug her out unscathed.

From the first, even when a young puppy, we left Brandy in the kitchen while we went off to work. At first we came home at lunch, made ourselves soup and toast, let the dog out, put her back, returned to the university. We thought nothing of it. Neither did we ask what the dog thought of it!

It seemed to be all fine, so when Brandy reached the age of responsibility, we left her all day, having our own lunch of chips and peas in the university Middle Common Room. We thought nothing of that either. It was a matter of needs must. We were busy people with careers to make.

Maybe we should not have had a dog in the first place; maybe the dog should not have had us. But we were all happy, we loved Brandy, Brandy – good natured soul that she was – loved us back. They were idyllic times, times that were made by our little companion and friend.

And, like all idylls, those times would come, soon enough, to an end.

The cottage, as I said, was rather blissfully isolated. It was that very isolation that caused the cottage to also become a threat.

First, Brandy discovered early one Saturday morning, (and to our great good fortune made friends with), a large man in our shrubbery. He was wet, cold, smelly and dishevelled. With

Brandy eagerly dancing about and yelping a welcome to her new friend he was ushered into the kitchen where he was provisioned with a mug of tea alongside a breakfast of two eggs, served up with our last slices of bacon and fried-bread.

It was a good thing that Brandy's generous nature had decided that the animal in the shrubbery was not a big version of the resident fox, but a human to be befriended rather than barked at. It turned out he had been released two day's earlier from Edinburgh's Saughton jail, having served out in full his six-year term for unprovoked Grievous Bodily Harm.

Second, Chris came home when I was away in the south of England to find the door smashed to smithereens and the house ransacked. (She and Brandy had gone to stay with her mother.) What few removable possessions we had were gone, stolen.

After that we lived in a permanent state of unease, and I could not contemplate leaving Chris alone in the gamekeeper's cottage, idyllic or not. Given my line of work, Chris being left alone would be inevitable. We would have to find somewhere safer to live, in a village perhaps, where there would be other people about.

*****

We needed a rather small van to move what goods and chattels we had left to the beautiful country village of Kirkwhelpington, to dwell for a few short, wonderful years amongst its generous-hearted north Northumbrian country natives. We rented a charming little house (Orchard House) in a farm labourer's cottage row, bang in the middle of the village. Kirkwhelpington was not a big place – *all* the houses were in the middle of the village. In front of each of the really old ones (like ours), was a field sufficient to graze a cow, and behind was another little field with outbuildings. We had found another patch of heaven on Northumberland's good earth.

It was twice as far away from the university as Blagdon had been, fully 35 minutes in our gallantly stuttering red Mini, or a bit longer on the local bus when the car was having one of its seizures.

Brandy was not yet to be released from her daily routine – five days a week – of being left in the morning with a toy filled with biscuits for her to worry at, to be there nine hours later to joyfully welcome us home; tail going, yapping with excitement, rushing round in circles. For us, first thing, take the dog out for a run; second job, light the fire to get some warmth back into the place; third job, Brandy's supper; fourth job, our supper (tinned meatballs, powdered potato, dried peas, followed by angel delight whisked up with water).

Orchard House had a most effective natural ventilation system. The outside fresh air came in under the door, through the living room and out up the chimney. On getting home of an evening we would be greeted with a trail of dead leaves right across the living room floor.

On the positive side, for Brandy there was plenty of outside semi-wild space for her to busy-about in. Next door was good value too, always worth a visit to see what scraps had been hurled out of the back door! Weekends were filled with long walks in north Northumberland's magnificent countryside and swims in the river Wansbeck. Brandy was at the very centre of our attention for all the time that we were home. The three of us. Brandy being the perfect excuse for going places to walk.

*****

Brandy was the first time our home life was wrapped up with a non-working dog. It was a new experience for us; getting full value from it was something we needed to learn. Brandy taught us. For the dog, her experience with us was much the same. Brandy's life was a life with us. She did not have a life independent of us. We had not realised this element of mutual dependency, it was a new idea – that a dog did not have a life independent of its carers.

Was this over-parenting? It certainly had not been the case on the farm. There, the terriers lives were sometime with us (if they chose), and sometime without us. They were carefree in both senses of the word – free to do their own thing, free of being cared for. The farm dogs ran loose. If we did not know where they were we did not much mind unless they missed their supper. In that case they were likely up to mischief.

But then our own parents did not seem to mind much where we boys were either, provided we were back in time for *our* supper.

Until the 1980s, dogs had to be licensed. The fee had been the same since the century's beginning – 7/6 – which was a serious amount of money back then. By the time it was abolished, it was trivial. Being licensed however gave dogs a certain status not possessed by the (unlicensed) cat. A run-over dog had to be reported by the car driver to the police. A run-over cat did not. The need for a license brought with it a note on the register, which meant the dog and its owner were known to the authorities; so there were responsibilities to be upheld with regard to controlling the dog.

None of this applied to the farm dogs. I do not remember ever getting any of our farm dogs licensed – including those that lived in the house. Farmers were well known for shooting each other's dogs and for that matter anybody else's dogs. The law was (still is) that any dog seen to be 'worrying' livestock, or thought to have worried livestock, or thought to be about to worry livestock, could be shot, without any further question. The culprits were usually dogs in pairs, the most frequent offenders being a sheepdog coupled with a terrier.

The sixties saw a change in the attitude expected by dog owners toward their dogs. Owners could no longer let their dogs have a life freely roaming about the countryside. A dog had to be under control at all times.

We took on this responsibility toward Brandy quite naturally, because she was the third member of the family and we wanted her with us all the time. Anyway, she was good company – fun to be with. But it was a general trend as well, one that went along with the depopulation of the countryside, more and more people living not on farms but in suburbia. The suburban dog used to be a rarity, by the seventies it had become a commonplace. And with that trend came the toy dogs, the lap dogs, the sad over-parented under-worked golden retrievers and collies.

Our village life at Kirkwhelpington was filled in the winter with evenings of stick-dressing (Tuesdays) and country-dancing (live fiddle and piano, Thursdays), Sunday, church. The village even had its own post office – one of those sort that sold custard cream biscuits and cans of Heinz baked beans. Summer weekend days were spent with the three of us, Chris, Brandy and me, wandering in the woods and fields around Kirkwhelpington and through the back lanes to Wallington Hall at Cambo.

Brandy was a great swimmer and never tired of leaping into the Wansbeck to chase after sticks splashed into the river for her. That dog would take to the water anywhere, criss-crossing rivers with gleeful yaps. This could be alarming if the water in question was wider or swifter than the Wansbeck. Loch

Sunart, for example, was a mite too wide for her to cross, but she survived (though I got very wet wading out after her!).

Chris stopped working to spend all day at home when she was six months pregnant. The family was about to be increased in number to four! Chris spent much of her time on an Imperial typewriter bashing out my research papers. At first Brandy deeply resented having her private daily space invaded by interlopers. She had got used to her weekdays alone.

Nonetheless, as is the way of all good dogs, Brandy kept faith with us, even if we had not kept faith with her. It must have been hard for Brandy when she was displaced by our firstborn – Brandy was no longer the centre of our undivided attention.

She took Joanna into her own. The good thing was that Brandy would never again be spending her days waiting for us to come home to her.

It turned out that Chris would not be going back to work (with me ever more frequently away abroad, she was full-time homemaker and mother – and to boot, part-time father as well). None of our dogs would be left alone in the way that Brandy had been. But she never seemed to have minded her previoius five consecutive days of nine hours' vigil in the kitchen at the gamekeeper's cottage waiting for us to re-appear. She did not develop any bad habits or traits indicative of mental anguish for being left alone all day in this way. She was the most well balanced of little dogs. Despite our bad behaviour towards her, she had come to no harm.

The only misfortune to befall Brandy was her predisposition to false pregnancies. These were most realistic. Her appetite increased, her abdomen swelled, milk began to flow into her mammary glands, signs of onset of parturition would become apparent. But never any puppies. Brandy would become quite distressed at this and would cool down only when the milk in her udder began to go away. After a series of false pregnancies we decided to have her spayed. The operation was bungled. Brandy got peritonitis; it nearly killed her.

As far as Brandy was concerned, the lovely thing about Chris being home all the day with our new baby daughter was that the walks around the Northumberland countryside were no longer restricted to weekends. Brandy was out and about every day. Brandy, Chris and the pram. The bond between dog and mistress that had begun at their first meeting was strengthened by the combined enterprise of baby caring. The baby was a joint effort; mother and dog.

In the event, the party that had been displaced in the family's affairs by the coming of our daughter was not the dog, it was the husband!

$$*****$$

Village life at Kirkwhelpington continued for another year before, with great regret, we had to go further north. Up to Edinburgh where the university had given me a permanent post. Something that I, as a family-man with a wife, dog and child to support, desperately needed.

There would be compensations. We bought our first house (correction: we took out a mortgage at 18% interest rate), 115 Main Street, Pathhead (for £3,000, which seems cheap, but my university salary was £980 p.a.). Our pride and joy was a 'semi', right on the main A68 trunk road from Edinburgh, south through the village. We moved there with the help of a local Kirkwelpington farmer's cattle truck – used earlier that same day and not very well hosed out after.

The house at Pathhead had loose slates on its roof (I fixed them back with well-chewed chewing gum), gently rotting window frames (which continued to rot undisturbed), woodworm in the roof (ditto), a kitchen with a cooker and a stone sink in it, living room and bedroom facing to the rear, front room and smaller bedroom facing the street. The entrance door was about three metres away from the traffic-filled road. Pathhead is on a hill slope. Just outside our house the lorries had to change down a gear which meant that the house shook and the noise penetrated every nook and cranny. There was nowhere to hide!

Chris's mother helped us move. She was aghast seeing the appalling place that her daughter (and granddaughter) were now expected to call home! But for us it was the first house that was ours to own, so it was just wonderful.

Pathhead was very different to the rural peace of Kirkwhelpington. But there was a garden (of sorts) leading onto a back lane by which you (and your dog) could get out into the neighbouring countryside without needing to battle with the lorries on the main road. That back path was a godsend for all the houses along Main Street. We called it Dogmuck Lane.

The other half of our semi-detached was occupied by a charming couple. She stayed home while he (now close to retirement) drove holiday coach trips around Scotland. In the early seventies, going on coach tours to Bonnie Scotland was the then-equivalent of jetting off to the Costa del Sol.

Mr and Mrs Brown took a shine to Brandy. Come what may, every time Brandy was let out into the back garden she would be round yapping at their door, upon which she would be let in and given treats of meat scraps kept specially for her. We could not compete; we ourselves ate all of what little meat we were able to buy!

Life progressed quietly until Chris held onto her third pregnancy to bring forth our second born. With daughter Jo and now son Jon to take care of, the house at Pathhead had become too small. Besides, its location was hardly the spot to bring up a growing family! The house had however tripled in value and had a willing buyer (bearing bundles of Scottish five-pound notes).

We could put a deposit down for a mortgage on a small new-build in West Linton, in the Pentland Hills. Detached, big garden surrounding, wooded bank behind, in a grouping of twenty just on the outskirts of the village. Our house was in the back corner under the shelter of the steep bank. At the bank top was a small green hill populated by grazing sheep and heifers. Perfect in every way – even if initially Rowancroft, Bogsbank Road, was a little on the small side.

This time we were moved with our (slightly increased) worldly goods and chattels roped onto the flat-bed lorry belonging to Mr Scougall (Coal Merchant, Pathhead). I'm not sure he ever got paid, but he'd have likely refused it anyway. Same as the farmer who moved us up from Kirkwhelpington. People seemed to do lots of things just out of goodheartedness back then.

For Brandy, life at West Linton was a return to the halcyon days of Kirkwhelpington. We still live there to this day. The village even has the river Lyne running right through the middle of it. But back then, I now had a happy family of Chris, two kids, and contented little prick-eared, bright-as-a-button, stubby-waggy-tailed dog. For the first three, thank you Chris. For the last one, thank you Brenda.

Brenda it was too who lent us (we never paid it back) £450 to buy the wooded bank to the rear of our garden. It was ever so nice to have it safe as the backdrop to our family house. It turned out, however, to be not so much 'nice-to-have' as a masterstroke of forward planning. For the wooded bank joined our garden with the fields beyond and there is no law of trespass in Scotland!

And thus it continued. At West Linton there was space enough for dog walks in every direction – straight from the house. Up into the hills, along the river, whatever. Brandy had five years of good life at West Linton before slowly falling apart. Her demise was gradual, and in the end pathetic for so lively and energetic a little dog.

Brandy lost her hearing first, which didn't seem to matter much because obedience was never her strong point. Then her sight. But she ate well enough and could see sufficient to keep up with our walks (not so difficult – the pace was set by the smallest child). Even her ever-progressing senility could be coped with for a little while, though it was distressing when Brandy would charge off looking for us in entirely the wrong direction. She never did take kindly to the lead.

We started talking about 'the proper kindness', 'the right thing to do', 'putting her out of her misery'. It was not something that had ever bothered me at the farm. The matter would (or would not) be discussed, the decision would be made. Father would take the .22 pistol from out the desk drawer, put two bullets in his pocket, go and do the right thing. We only ever heard one *crack*. The second bullet went back in the drawer with the gun – ready for next time.

But this was different. This was *our little family dog*, the first one we had had. She had been with us for all but one of our young married years together, the years we were making our family – with the dog a full part of it. Through trial and tribulation, good times and bad, she was part of us. We could not get up courage enough to face our duty to our best wee friend.

She got an ear infection and she could not fight it. It went rapidly into her inner ear and Brandy lost her sense of balance and started blundering about. Antibiotics would fix it – Chris would take her to the vet. Man that I was, I left Chris to it, volunteering to stay home to look after the kids.

Chris had lifted little square Brandy up on to the table at the veterinary surgery for the vet to look at her. The vet, however, instead chose to look at Chris with a questioning eye. Chris it was who found the courage, but only for two seconds.

'I think you'd better put her down.'

Her words pierced her. She could not bear that she had said it. The poor little dog. She burst into floods of tears. Distraught, she stumbled out of the surgery, running to the car, howling in anguish. Brandy was left with the vet, standing alone on his cold metal table, with a suppurating ear, unable to hear, unable to see, unable to understand … abandoned, alone.

I'm sure the vet was very kind. Brandy never did come back home. There is no grave for her in our garden as for the other dogs, no daffodils above her, no crocus to signal spring.

Chris sobbed all the way home, and for long after. She had not been there where she should have been, to comfort her little dog at the last. She could not bear it. Nor was I there for Brandy; she was my dog too. Nor was I there for Chris. Neither of us have been able to forgive ourselves for such wretchedly bad behaviour. It weighs heavy upon us to this day. Just a little dog with an eager face, prick ears and a happy tail.

It was all very tough. We had loved that dog so much more than we ever knew while we had her. The children had known Brandy every day of their lives. Brandy had been there for them for ever, they knew of no life that did not have the wee dog in it.

The end had been so hard that we vowed we could not go through it again.

We would *never* have another dog.

Our animals teach us the hard lessons.

Recovering from Loss

By this time, I had finally severed all links with the old family farm by asking my brother to buy me out of my 'fourth' share. The realised sum was rather little! But in truth, I had left the place a number of years earlier.

Little though it might have been, my fourth share was sufficient to purchase outright the fourteen acres of gentle hill to the west of our house that was bounded by the glebe on one side and our wooded bank on the other. A sharp climb up the bank gave us direct access from our back door via the garden to the field.

We installed a gate at the top of the bank. A zig-zag path was made traversing across the slope to wind its way up the fifty-foot of rise, from garden at the bottom up to the field gate at the top. A stable was built near the field's access gate. The girls' ponies were duly turned out into the grazing paddocks. We extended the house to give us a utility room, another two rooms and a shower.

Brandy having so admirably set her family up for phase one of their lives, we were now ready for phase two. The phase of sophistication.

Young (well, reasonably), upwardly mobile, mid-career, boringly unbearably on top of the job. The era of dinner parties, yew-veneer dining-room tables, trips into Edinburgh for the posh hairdressers, Pony Club at weekends for the three children, chickens for outdoor eggs, pet rabbits in the hutch on the lawn, guinea pigs in the shed, hamsters in the bedroom, fish in the tropical tank, cats by the (ersatz) fire, television in the living room, built-in dish-washer and fridge, Volvo in the drive, early to work, late home, two double whiskies before supper of an evening, ulcers in the stomach … and a *fashionable* dog.

Bella (… *Bella?!*) was a long-haired miniature dachshund. Entirely unsuited to our way of life, but absolutely *à la mode*. We got her from a smart lady in a swanky house at the poshest end of a fashionable Edinburgh suburb. We got Bella because every household/family should have its dog, and because we could not get used to the place without Brandy around. Brandy was a small dog with a large personality who filled a big space. We could not stand that empty space.

Bella proved to be far from up to Brandy strength. Bella was, well, Bellissima … Petite, with silky long black and tan hair, long dangly ears, long nose, long imperious tail. She was regal in her walk – in her early years anyway. Not being a natural investigator, she was happy on the lead. She was happiest however on the sofa, in the car, by the radiator. Sad-eyed beautiful Bella was no great excitement for anybody. Fortunately, while Brandy had been part of the children's younger lives, by Bella's time there were more important things to occupy and interest them: bikes, horses, friends, fighting with each other. But she kept Chris company in the garden and up the field.

Bella met her end by being galloped by one of the children's horses. It was cold-blooded, violent murder. Horses are mostly indifferent to dogs, but little ones can spook them. In this case however the horse concerned simply held a grudge: he had had it in for Bella and caught her in an unguarded moment.

She saw him too late, coming for her at the gallop, and she was too slow to dodge. A dog being galloped by a full-on head down charging horse is a most disturbing event. On this occasion, it was witnessed by Chris and our young son (whose dislike of horses was fulsomely confirmed). A horse knows precisely where its hooves are going, even at the gallop. That is how horses of goodwill can so deftly avoid trampling on their fallen riders. In Bella's case the hooves were aimed with lethal accuracy. Chris was in shock. Jon picked up the broken body and brought Bella back down to the house. There was nothing the vet could do.

Dear Chris, whose love of animals far outstrips her love for the human race, had now been at the epicentre of two consecutive tragic events surrounding the loss of her best friends. It was not fair. It was at least a blessing that when Bella was lost we already had Sam, with whom Chris had a special bond. Chris shared her sorrow with Sam, and they were both inconsolable.

Bella did do one notably good thing (other than look beautiful). She got pregnant. Getting dogs and horses pregnant is a common solution to not being able to think of much else to do with the animal. Unfortunately the end purpose of pregnancy, giving birth, was not Bella's forte. Her efforts were less than robustly rustic, as might perhaps befit her delicate sensitivities. The first pregnancy, after some effete attempts at labour, produced one live puppy. Following this wholly unsatisfactory event we were given a free re-mating. This was a disastrous mistake. A Caesarean yielded two dead puppies out of a toxic uterus. We promised ourselves never to try to breed from any of our dogs again. Indeed, we vowed never to have another bitch; that vow, like all the others, we did not keep.

Bella's one live puppy from her first litter had struggled its way through early life to make a reasonably sturdy eight-week-old. This at least Bella had done, and she had done it very well indeed. She made two old ladies happy for many a year to come after.

Back in Cheshire, Brenda had lost her dog. Samatha had lived to a ripe old age, outliving her daughter. By now, Brenda had left the farm (there was nothing there to stay for) and was living with her sister. They too had been a household of three. The loss of Samatha left both the ageing sisters bereft. Bella it was who resolved their plight with her single outstanding success, Bessie. We took little Bessie down to the sisters and simply gave the little puppy to them.

They doted on that little dog. When Brenda's sister died, Bessie became Brenda's sole companion. When Bessie finally died, Brenda could no longer live in the house without her. She voluntarily moved into an old people's home. There are no dogs in old people's homes. It is wrong to call them *homes*.

*****

Our 'country life' had evolved into what was to be its lasting form. Farm life had become village life, then, with our own small hill right there, with the gate through to the twisting path down the wooded bank into our garden, and we were back to our rural roots, although rather better ordered than the dairy farm had been.

The field was big enough for the hens to be moved up there – the flock increased by the purchase of twelve point-of-lay pullets. The stables were extended to handle two horses over-wintered inside, a hay shed, a pony shelter and a tack room. The vegetable garden was relocated up there too, nearer the midden with its now copious quantities of rotting horse manure (nothing better). The field was divided into three so the horses could be rotated with the sheep (twelve of those – hand-sheared, Dyffryn-style) and with Wendy, our charming gentle Belted Galloway coo, who would be joined, in due time, by the brother's goat.

Further thoughts of maintaining any pretence of sophistication were quashed not just by the animals, or the filthy state of the utility room, or the twice daily climb up the bank taking us through into the field. It was the teenagers; they didn't do sophistication.

Bella had done sophistication though. Bella had settled to life as a house and garden dog; finding a fellow-being in the Siamese cat. Bella did not do walks. The house bit was fine, Bella fitted in. She was nice to have about the place, rather like the cat.

But there was more to be had out of life in West Linton, set at one thousand feet, surrounded by the south Pentland Hills. There was walking to be done. And the field to be enjoyed. Bella did not much enjoy either: perhaps she had had a premonition.

When the youngest (third child, second daughter) was left perfectly happy at the door for her first day at the village Primary School, Chris returned to a house that lacked what Brandy had provided. With no child there any more it was empty. Anyway, what was she going to do with her days now? Hoover?

'We need a proper dog. A dog for the field. A proper walking dog.'

'Another Brandy?'

'Hmmm … '

'There are some long-haired daxy puppies in the local paper. That would make a pair, Bella would have a companion. They would be walked out together. A pair of proud daxys. You would cut quite a dash with them.'

'Let's go and look.'

We went to a rather nice house set above the Tweed at Dryburgh. The owner of the litter of eight sweet little dachshund pups was quite charming. The pups were horrendously expensive. We put our name down for the only one left, a little girl.

'They were lovely, weren't they?'

'Hmmm… I'm not sure. It's not us any more. They're too twee. Too wee. Too fancy-pants. Don't we need something, well, a little more "robust"? Brandy was a tough little nut. Up for anything. Terrier.'

'When you think about it, maybe we need something bigger. I need something to do when I've dropped Emma off to school. The likes of Bella need taking for a walk; and then they sort of resent it. They feel it is their duty to do you a favour and come with you. I need somebody who will take *me* for a walk. Demand that I take them out. Otherwise, I'm going to turn into a couch potato like Bella.'

'If the miniature long-haired dachshund isn't "us", then what is "us"?'

'Bigger! Always fancied a sheepdog!'

'No sheepdogs! They have to be worked. We don't have work for a working dog. A sheepdog would go mad.'

We had a fortnight before the new acquisition of a very pretty, very expensive, long-haired miniature dachshund bitch was to be picked up. In that fortnight a few things happened.

The village held its annual week of festivities – as is customary hereabouts – the Border Festivals and Common

Ridings. Every town and village has one. Everybody goes. Our next-door neighbour of a few years past, having flitted to live in the wilds of the Pentlands hinterland, was down in the village to join in. She was sporting a generous selection of her many children and a rather nice dark golden retriever dog. Not one of the heavy lumbering domestic kind, but a lightweight country working dog.

'That's a super dog. We thought you had dachshunds?'

They used to have – we knew that well enough – a smooth-haired standard by the name of Puffin. We knew all about Puffin. We were attacked by a frantically barking Puffin every time we went out of our drive. He would rampage in front of his own house and shout at us, every bark accompanied by his ears flying skyward and his front legs coming off the ground.

'Oh no! Not after Puffin. No more daxys. We've had these retrievers for a while now. Our bitch has just had puppies. They're about four weeks old. She's had so many I don't know what to do with them all. Come over and have cup of tea. See them. They're lovely.'

We did. They were.

Irresistibly lovely warm licky squashy happy golden bundles. We chose a dog. He would be a 'proper' dog. He was named even before we got him home: Sam.

We phoned the ever-so-nice people at Dryburgh. We were duly apologetic. They were frostily nice and we felt bad. But it was a good decision.

Within a day of Sam's arrival to his new home, we were off to the Queen's Garden Party at Holyrood, invited to join Her Majesty's pleasure on her summer holiday in Edinburgh. We left eight-week-old Sam in the care of the kids. When we got back we knew we had a proper family dog with us again. Sam had already endeared himself to the children. He would be their dog too, part of our family, one of the gang.

Bella did not mind in the least. She was no longer the centre of attention, she was allowed to get on with her day undisturbed and it suited her just fine. She was never a bouncy dog. At best her tail would wag slowly, lady-like. She didn't enthuse much. She did however become fond of Sam, and would even deign to play games with him when she was so minded. Sam was besotted with her; he thought Bella was just wonderful! We did not actually realise the extent to which Sam had bonded to Bella until we lost Bella in those tragic and upsetting circumstances. Sam mourned the loss of his friend and fell into a deep depression. Before that sad day however, Bella and Sam would have four happy years together.

Sam did indeed take Chris for walks, long walks, every day while the kids were at school. Chris and Sam spent their days exploring the West Linton countryside with each other. She felt safe with him and he looked after her.

He would welcome the children back home from school with huge wide tail wags, knocking over flower vases, ornaments and everything else that had not already been put out of reach.

Sam grew to be a big dog. They played together, the children and Sam. He was a no-problem dog. He just did everything we did. Coming along, trotting ahead, leading the way. We all loved Sam to bits, especially Chris, and our feelings were reciprocated. Sam was a seriously lovely dog who could do everything, go anywhere.

Sam had the habit of going on a dozen or so paces ahead of us then turning his head to check that we were all keeping up behind. He quite liked to be on a lead when bidden, it gave him proximity to the person he loved the most – his mistress. Sam never pulled (unless a deer crossed the path) or dragged. On the lead he liked to trot alongside, the perfect Gentleman.

He enjoyed himself in our company and we in his, on ordinary days, on holidays in the country and at the beach, on adventures over the hills. The best sort of family dog.

*****

Different dogs require different things of their owners. Sheepdogs: sheep. Terriers: rats. Hounds: foxes. Gundogs: game. Lapdogs: laps.

Likewise, different owners require different things of their dogs.

The illogicality of human behaviour comes to the fore all too readily in the matter of dogs. It is more often 'Wouldn't it be nice to have a …' when it should have been 'What do we want a dog to do for us?'

Throughout our lives, Chris and I have been different people with a different family with different wants. To our great good fortune more often than not we were able to match our needs with the needs of our dog. These were good times, valued above all others. For the dog, lasting only for its life; but for us, lasting forever. That is why my ageing mother was so desperate to know that she would meet her dogs after she had died. I hope she did and I hope we do.

That perfect match was achieved with Brandy. It was there again for us, with Sam. When our lives entered the post-bedlam stage that came when the four children grew up and left home, we would manage it a wonderful three more times in a row. Maybe we just got sensible.

Sam was perfect for the family we had when we had him, a household so chaotic that the dog had to be a part of it in a seamless 'look after yourself and don't be a bother' sort of way. We never had to worry about Sam, he was always just there, being big friendly tail-waving Sam. Sam was not clever, Sam was not stupid, Sam was a retriever. He was just friendly; generous, broad-headed, soft-coated, floppy eared, wet-nosed, sloppy-tongued.

*****

Horse people are usually dog people. It goes with the lifestyle, with the frame of mind, and if the dog is lucky, with ample access to run around in space.

It is a conflicting predilection however, because horses and dogs do not usually much like each other.

Dogs seem unaware of the dangers. The horse on the other hand seems incapable of delivering a soft reprimand to a pesky dog fooling around its legs. Dogs bothering a goat, ewe or cow can be lucky enough to be admonished with sufficient pain inflicted only to give warning that better manners on the dog's part might be a good idea in the future. The horse however seems incapable of a warning stamp on the ground or a pulled punch with a hind leg. A dog kicked by a horse with steel shoes on its hooves is in danger of severe injury or worse. The best horse breakers have a stable yard full of dogs so the horses get used to them and become tolerant. Otherwise ...

The worst misdemeanour that a hunt follower can commit is for her (or his) horse to damage one of the precious hounds. Though fox hunting has four animals participating: fox, hound, horse, human, you will never see hunt followers on their horses out in the field ever mixing with the hounds. It is anathema. Errant riders on horses that get amongst the hounds are sent home and told not to bring that horse (and sometimes themselves) back again.

Pony and horse events are a riot of disorganisation, only falling into order when the horses are actually involved in some positive activity or other: dressage, cross country, jumping. Between times there is a chaotic mêlée. And in every horse-box cab, in every parent's Landrover, in every spectator's BMW there will be a dog. Pray that it stays there!

Sam loved the Pony Club events. He would come with Chris. He was the most well-behaved and accommodating chap. Everybody he met would be given his generous-headed wide-mouthed smile, his hello-wag. There would be no frenetic jumping about, only the sort of manners that would be expected of a country gent. He was always on a lead, beside Chris. At the walk, standing patiently, sitting quietly watching all the goings on.

There was no downside to Sam. What a blessing that we had turned down that long-haired miniature! Golden retrievers are probably the shortest living of dogs. We expected eight years would be the most that we would be privileged to share with Sam in our family. He lived to be fifteen. In his later years he struggled on round his field every day with us. As each day went by it became more difficult, but he would be there come what may.

It was Sam's field really. The fourteen acres of green hill is a glorious mixture of nature's gifts. At a thousand feet it is unusually sandy – the hill actually being a sand and gravel moraine deposited by the retreating Ice Age glacier. It is a paradise for dogs, with space to run and bounce. Space to hunt for mice in the long grass, every new morning with the smells of fox, badger, stoat and weasel, naughty rabbits to chase until they cheat by disappearing miraculously into the ground. Pheasant to put up and watch clatter away, the noise of the geese skeining overhead to bark at, grass tussocks hiding the meadow pipit's nest, little holes leading to the dry grassy balls that are the homes of vole and shrew, profusions of pasture flowers wafting wild fragrances, interestingly investigable buzzy bees hiding in their nodding heads.

Sam loved the field above all else. Being there was what he did with his mistress every day without fail. He struggled round it to the last. On that last morning we knew he had had enough. He had just got too old to cope. He would not get round for another day.

Sam was put down in his bed in the utility room. Both Chris and I were with him. He is buried in his field, halfway up the slope over which he would so joyfully bound. We pass his place every day of our lucky lives. So have all the dogs we have had since Sam. I wonder if they know that the patriarch lies there, happily grinning with his tongue lolling out and waving his tail.

*****

Poppy had come to help Sam recover from his loss of Bella. In that single regard she did well enough. In retrospect, Poppy was not really such a sensible decision and overall, she was a bit of a disappointment. I suppose we can blame soft-centred Sam for Poppy. When Bella was taken so violently from us, Sam did not understand. Dogs know when their mates are getting old and near death. If they are allowed to see their old friend die and smell that he is no longer there, there is a chance that the mourning will be matter-of-fact and brief. They will miss their chum to be sure, but they will get on with their lives as any dog does.

That did not happen for Sam. He must have been very fond of Bella, in a way that opposites attract, I guess. Sam grieved over Bella with an intensity that put him into a deep depression from which he seemed to be unable to recover, despite our best efforts to occupy him and distract him. He would not eat. He was starving himself into a decline.

In a moment of madness Chris took charge of matters. As it turned out, her actions *did* resolve Sam's state of depression. The puppy that was Poppy fully commanded Sam's avuncular instincts. It was about the only thing Poppy ever got right.

Chris and our (then) youngest daughter took themselves off to Portobello, to the Dog Rescue Centre. There they met a sweet little puppy of indeterminate age. They said twelve weeks – well, what other age would a puppy be that was wanted rid of? They had the temerity to charge £20.

Home she came. Naturally!

From the beginning the children called her 'Puppy-dog'. So it stuck, 'Poppy-dog'.

Poppy was firstly a bitch (we had decided after Bella no more bitches; we spayed Poppy). She was of indeterminate provenance, but she was promised (by the kennel maid) to be a small dog. Well, what other size would a dog be that was wanted rid of? Poppy turned out bigger than a Welsh collie; she was also black and white with a sheepdog face and ears. There was something else there too … just mongrel.

Poppy was a nice puppy, bit slow to get house trained perhaps, but Sam loved her, and that was the idea after all. Poppy the puppy entranced Sam, who decided his mission in life was to look after her. Within days he was back to his usual old 'Gentleman Retriever' self.

Poppy had nine or ten fairly colourless years with us. She got up in the morning. Chased rabbits up the field. Ate her breakfast and tea. Slept in the utility room with Sam. Herded the odd hen about. Didn't take to being trained, but was never badly behaved. We couldn't work out why she was so 'distant'.

Emotionally flat. We found by chance that Poppy was absolutely terrified – petrified – of black bin bags. Upon sight or sound of a black bag in our hands she would cringe, whine, slink off and hide. Putting two and two together I reckoned Poppy and her other unwanted siblings had been piled into a black plastic bag, tied by the neck. Destined I guess for chucking into the Lochrin Basin of the Edinburgh Union canal. Someone funked it and just dumped the bag, only to be found later, its contents duly delivered to the place where all such foundlings end up, the Dog Rescue Centre. Poppy showed all the symptoms of an early-life bout of oxygen deficit – she was somewhat short of brain cells.

Poppy was not a very doggy dog. But we had her, Sam had her, and for Poppy a life with us was better than no life. Poppy was so unpretentious that she would get ignored, forgotten about, left by mistake in the house while the family went out. Even left forgotten in the car while we went walks in the hills.

'Hey, where's Poppy?'

'Was she with us?'

'She was in the car!'

'That was three hours ago!'

'It'll be OK, she'll be there when we get back!'

And so she always was.

Poppy became, really quite early on, demented. It was not so much that she became 'forgetful'. She behaved irrationally. She did not know where she was, what she was trying to do. She drove us all crazy. Her demented behaviour made her totally unmanageable. She developed into a most unhappy dog. I think she was pleased when she went. The ultimate sadness is that Poppy left no discernible hole in our family life.

Poor silly Poppy; she did no harm.

Dogs Shared

Midge came for Emma. Emma was the third – and we promised ourselves last – human addition to the family. She was spoilt like all last and youngest children should be, specially if they are little girls. Then, at the age of nine, her life at the centre of everybody's attention was rudely shattered. Becca arrived! Emma had (still has) a close, caring, relationship with her younger sister which has lasted through the years. Emma's problem wasn't Becca, it was us! It wasn't just that a young baby and then a toddler naturally command more of their parents attention than an adolescent making her way successfully through school. It was also the case that, of all the children, Becca was quite demanding, filling a lot of emotional space. Or maybe it was us, showing our age!

Whatever, we wanted to do something for Em, so she would know that she was still special. And what makes you feel special in the world? Your dog! What Emma needed was her own special dog. That would be Midge. Midge was a very particular kind of special dog.

*****

We were with Emma at the Horse Trials (three-day event), at Thirlstane. We had gone there to see Jo who had got her horse into the BHS Novice Class that was held the day before Dressage Day of the main event. All the international professionals were there – the big names like Ian Stark, Ginny Leng, Mary King –with their young horses, bringing them on. Jo had done a great job of taming the terror that was her first pony – Cammy – into a good eventer at Regional Pony Club level. Now she had moved up with a Thoroughbred. We bought Meadow-Brown as a youngster, barely broken to the saddle, never mind trained. Jo had put hour after hour into Meadow-Brown, who was now fit to enter the big time. I had never seen a young horse perform a Dressage Test the way Jo got Brown to do.

We had watched, fascinated, to see Mark Todd from New Zealand sweat with the effort of putting a young rookie mare through her paces in the dressage ring, and were now off to see the Cross-Country.

Being a horse event, the place was, as ever, covered in dogs. Big dogs, little dogs, posh dogs, farmyard dogs. Jack Russells by the barrowload.

'Look at that Mum!' Emma was gesticulating, 'I want a dog like that! That's the one I want! Isn't he fine!'

My stomach sank, I had caught sight of the bloodhound slobbering about the place earlier on in the day.

'Where dear, which one do you mean?'

'There!'

We could see nothing.

'There! The daxy! Look!'

And there indeed was a miniature smooth-coated dachshund, tummy just clear of the grass, tail erect, ears down, head up. Proud as punch. Four square body, leg at each corner, deep wide chest, shoulder and thigh muscles bulging. Bigger by far than any soppy bloodhound.

'What a fine fellow!' we muttered. 'Stand back, Em, there's a horse coming on down the track, going for the water.'

And that was the end of that.

Within the week, Chris was on the case. An advert in the pets section of *The Scotsman* said there was a litter, eight weeks old, ready to go. An Edinburgh phone number.

'Hello, Oh yes, that'll be my husband. He is up in Lochinver.'

'Where?'

'Up north, Assynt. What's your telephone number, I'll tell him to give you a ring.'

We looked at the map. It was impossible. Hours and hours away. It would take us two days to get there!

In the event, he rang and it was he who came down to us, not just from Assynt to their Edinburgh flat, but out to West Linton with the bitch and the remaining puppy. He was there for Emma when she came home from school; a birthday present. A bundle of energy from the start.

There was no distance too far for Midge, no obstacle too great to surmount, no threat that could not be beaten off. All these things, but mostly Midge was a friendly chap, enduringly faithful to his young mistress.

Midge got his name because he so small, midget. Soon after, that sort of nomenclature was considered socially unacceptable, so we made pretence that we had called him Midge because he was always busying about, like a midge – the renowned Scottish pesky. Midge *was* small, but it mattered not one whit: he could do everything the other dogs could do, and more. Midge was out in front.

Midge was not asked to sleep with the other dogs. Midge would have his bed in Emma's bedroom. Paddy had been my soul companion through difficult years in my young life, and he slept in his wicker chair in my room. He was there through the night, there in the morning, there when I was ill, and through the day, Paddy was with me whatever I was about. We wanted that for Emma.

On Midge's first night with us, the little chap was given a bed and a blanket on the floor in Emma's bedroom. Her puppy – she was the one who would be kept awake all night with pathetic abandoned-puppy whining. The bedroom floor was lined with paper, appropriate for a new puppy not yet in full control of his bladder and bowel. He was far too small to jump onto the bed.

But where was he next morning?

In Emma's bed!

He had been a cold, lonely puppy missing his mum. There was only one right place for him!

Sleeping *on* beds was strictly not allowed. So sleeping *in* beds was way out of line. Midge established his position in Emma's life right on day one. From the start, Midge slept in Emma's bed. He would be there every night Emma was home, in the bed, her constant companion.

Of course, Midge was a family dog too. Emma was at school through the day, and in later years away at university for twelve weeks at a time. Midge was part of the family when Emma was away, and part of Emma when she was home. When she was away Midge had to sleep with us, in our bedroom to be sure, but in his own bed. He had a humungous snore.

Midge was loyal to his mistress, just as Paddy had been to me.

Dogs have to endure, without resentment, the ups and downs of family life.

After university, Emma joined a research team at Edinburgh. While Emma was doing her research project, Midge was with us. He would go with Chris at lunchtime for them all to walk around the extensive Research Institute grounds together.

We thought the shepherd Emma had met while she was doing lambing work in the college Easter vacation was a passing phase. He wasn't. Emma went to live with him in a small cottage out in Midlothian country, leaving Chris and I, her family house, and all its dogs. Including little Midge.

There were sheepdogs a-plenty about the shepherd's cottage. But to him, only working dogs counted; he had time only for his sheepdogs, which he kept in kennels, set up the road away from the cottage. He did not want dogs in the house, especially small, independent ones.

Not for the first time would a man taking up residence be resentful of his girlfriend's dog. Men are often jealous of competition for a girl's affection; three being a crowd in the household, never mind in the bed. And not for the first time would a woman try to assert: 'Love me? Then love my dog'. The wise man, loving the girl, will love also the girl's dog but Emma's partner wanted her little dog out of his house.

So Midge lived with us.

As time went by, Emma's relationship with her shepherd went even more sour. To try to compensate for her ever more difficult circumstances, Emma, with our encouragement, took Midge away from us once more to live with her and her partner. But it did not work.

Midge was as desperately unhappy as his mistress. Emma could not leave. But Midge could. Emma brought Midge back again to me and Chris, to be safe and happy. And there she left him.

Emma came frequently back our house, her old home, bringing their young son Daniel with her. Midge was there for them with a welcome always ready. Midge might have been shared, but he never forgot it was Emma who was his mistress.

Midge stayed with us, enjoying a busy family life for a few more years until he was taken with ever more frequent fits. These were agony for the proud little dog and he howled in a most distressing way. Initially we would comfort and quiet him and, after a lie down, he would recover to be his usual self. But the fits got worse. He was nearly fourteen years old.

We buried him below the oak tree in our garden, a garden which Midge had always loved. It is easy to know where he is buried. Every spring it is a mass of joyfully exuberant crocuses.

*****

It was only a year or so later that Chris caught Emma on her computer looking at the Kennel Club website. 'What are you looking for?'

'I want a dog, Mum. Daniel and I need a dog. Not a piece of farm equipment, not a sheepdog, I want a family dog. If I have a dog it will need to be Midge-sized. Small enough to come to work with me, to live in the car and go walks with me through the day.'

No more was said.

Both of them knew exactly what would fit the bill: a miniature wire-haired dachshund. Like the standard wire, the miniature wire daxy is not at all like the smooth or the long-haired variety. The wires come from a quite different origin, from the slightly larger hunting teckel. They are small, chunky, short-legged square-bottomed dynamos with floppy ears either side of a broad head, terrier jaw, bright eyes, tail proud.

A Kennel Club breeder had been located in Norton, over the river Derwent from Malton in deepest Yorkshire. There were puppies.

We arranged that Chris and I would call in on our way back from a summer holiday in the Yorkshire Dales. We misjudged how long it would take to cross Yorkshire using its rural byways but the young breeder was still there, waiting by her gate. She lived with her father in a small house on an estate. They had kennels at the bottom of their little garden where they looked after the rescue dogs that even the rescue centre would not have. He must've been rather unpopular with the neighbours! We had not quite expected the breeder to be so young a girl. She had her head well enough screwed on though, with an ambition to breed and show her dogs (an ambition she spectacularly realised with her wires).

We went inside to see first a kitchen, then a living room festooned with rosettes won at dog shows. This young lady knew what she was about – she meant business! We chose the puppy and brought him home, crying all the four hours of the journey on Chris's lap.

Emma's three-year-old son, Daniel, had called the tiny puppy 'my friend'. So Mungo was named after St Mungo, the Scottish patron saint whose name means 'friend'. Because of the sheepdogs at Emma's cottage, little Mungo could not go there till he was through all his vaccinations. So for the first couple of months he was our puppy. We thought he was great. He thought he was great! He had plenty of that teckel hunting blood in him.

It was quite apparent that Mungo relished his time when he was here with us and the other dogs, rousting about up in the field. What we named The Small Hill was his playground. The long grass with its native residents challenged Mungo's hound instincts. There was room to chase tennis balls and play with the other dogs – not least finding for them the balls they had lost.

The next five years saw Mungo living part time with us and our dogs at West Linton and part time at Emma's cottage. Mungo went on to see much sadness in his life – but a lot of happiness too. He was there for Emma when she finally took charge of her own life and found happiness. Mungo had hated the cottage that he should have been calling his home. The shepherd did not like him, and behaved just as he had done to Midge, and for the same reasons. He could not see it. Take the dog away from the girl: lose the girl.

In the inevitable end, Emma plucked up the courage to take control herself and rent a fully furnished place sufficiently nearby that Daniel could stay at his primary school for his last year.

In the new little rented cottage, Mungo had at last a happy place to share with his mistress and life improved enormously for them both. Mungo looked after Emma night and day as Emma gradually regained a life of something near normality and Mungo became as happy with her as was with us. He was doing a fine job. There were good walks to be had too.

With the exception of myself, who he had known since he was a puppy, Mungo had developed a deep fear of men. But when Michael (a globe-trotting poultry-industry consultant) appeared on the scene, Mungo saw no threat. Michael was happy to share Emma's affection.

Michael gave Emma both the love and the life she needed and Mungo was a part of a happy threesome. They bought a house near Daniel's secondary school.

Mungo was always happiest outdoors whenever he was with us, he loved the field so much. But indoors he was happiest with his mistress Emma. Later Michael and Emma's work often took them abroad so in Mungo's latter years he was as much with us as with them. He was a shared dog, and happy with that. We were especially fond of Mungo. He was such a good sport. Even in old age, beginning to feel the pain in his bones, Mungo would charge around the garden playing hide-and-seek.

*****

We have just left Mungo's grave. Freshly dug by Emma and Michael. They had brought him back to rest at last in his favourite place, the family's field – The Small Hill at West Linton.

Around were scattered a few handfuls of black soil, displaced by his small square rough-haired body. There was not much soil – Mungo was only little but he thought of himself as a wolfhound.

Emma and Michael's daughter was four years old when Mungo died. I wonder if she will remember him? I hope so. He was her stalwart friend, if occasionally a little grumpy and lacking the best of breath in his old age.

Mungo's departure left another large hole, this time in the middle of two families.

The more important a dog is to us, the more that dog is missed. It is not just the fun, the companionship, the faithful friendship that we mourn, it is a broken bond that runs deep. It is difficult to explain but it is to be wept over when lost.

Thank you Mungo. Feisty little Mung. You were a good wee dog. You were there for the difficult times. But you shared the good times too, and you helped to turn the shadows into sunshine.

The Colonel
and the Squaddie

On the wall in my study is a finely detailed wood carving, probably mid-late 1800s, from Innsbruck, given to my grandfather by his brother-in-law when they were young men on a skiing trip in the early 1900s. That was when you shouldered your skis to carry them up the mountain on foot, before skiing back down. It is of a Tyrolean shooting party leaving the hostelry for a day of sport with their game bags and firearms slung over their shoulders. The party has with them, on rope leads, their dogs, general purpose hounds for searching out, putting-up and tracking game. There is no question about it, those dogs are hunting teckels. They were in almost every respect the same as the modern wire-haired standard dachshund, although perhaps a little longer in the leg. Although dachshund ('*daxhunt*') translates to 'badger dog', there is no suggestion of their being used to tackle badgers in their setts.

*****

It was after Sam was gone. Chris was troubled by the empty space that Sam had left in all our lives. At a show at Larkhall, she and Emma had discovered that not all dachshunds were miniature, nor were all either long-haired like Bella, or smooth-haired like Midge.

Chris had gone there to see a breeder of miniatures, in our quest to find another Midge (impossible!). But she came away from Larkhall with an altogether different idea.

Emma had discovered the standard wire!

'Mum, come and look at these. They're amazing!' She had seen her first *proper* dachshund. A wire. 'What are they? Are they Dandy Dinmonts?'

The misattribution was excusable, for the Dandy Dinmont (before it was a called a Dandy Dinmont) was a rough-natured rough-haired terrier of standard dachshund-size local to the Scottish Borders. One of Walter Scott's characters was a farmer called Dandy Dinmont; he had them. So those dogs were Dandy Dinmonts.

At the dog show, the error was apparently unforgivable. A voice of protestation boomed from behind them, 'They are not! Indeed they are not. These are standard wire-haired dachshunds. They are a most ancient hunting and tracking hound.' Both Emma and Chris had been greatly taken.

This fellow was quite a big dog with deep red coarse hair. Resplendent in his thick coat, he sported a fine whiskery moustache, beard on his chin, tousled head, bushy eyebrows, long drooping hairy ears, and on his short muscled legs, fine red trousers. He stood four square, legs perpendicular under him.

The show-class at Larkhall was small and there were few breeders. The standard wire was a rarity, but Chris was smitten. That was what she wanted and nothing else was going to do. A telephone chase-about followed which ended up in north Wales. There was a bitch in pup at Holywell. Now that was a place I knew! It was only a stone's throw away from the old family farm. My uncle had even tried to farm there for a few years – at that time it was not even supplied with electricity or mains water (light was provided from a Tilly lamp, water from the pump at the cattle trough, and heat from the fire in the kitchen). It was a long way from West Linton.

My mother volunteered to investigate (anything to see a dog, especially a hound!). Her report was good. It was a big farmhouse, the bitch was good natured, laid back, flaming red, broad headed, big paws, friendly. Not so unlike a smaller version of her own wolfhounds, but with shorter legs.

Mother approved. She went again a couple of months later to choose the pup. It was not difficult: male, bold, healthy, and red. Becca and I went down in the Land Rover for a flying visit to Mother, then on to Holywell.

The puppy came back, as yet un-named, on Rebecca's lap. He was not happy. He whined (when he wasn't vomiting) all the way up, inconsolable at being separated from his mother, brothers and sisters. When he finally arrived back to his new home he howled the night through, making his presence felt right from the start.

It took a while to name him. We wanted his name to reflect not where he had come from, but where he would be spending his life. His coat was as red as any Highland Chieftain's. Even as a wee puppy he stood four-square, tail up, head up. He had the hugest, widest, softest, fattest, paddy-paws imaginable! He was one smart dog. So what else could he be called but Fergus, - first King of Scotland!

*****

Fergus was to become a most important part of Chris and my life.

He was born at the turn of the millennium. Three of our four children were away from the family nest, to a greater or lesser extent. The unrelenting hurricane that had been our household since Jo had been joined by Jon, Em and Becca, had (at last) abated.

My professional life had peaked, and I was looking forward to returning to a few more fun years as a Research Professor before retirement, while Chris could look back to her successful mothering of a family that was now making its way in the world. She had every reason to be proud to see that her years of caring had borne fruit.

Fergus however lost no time in letting us both know who would be the senior person in the household. Fergus would guide us by example into our retirement years. If something urgent was needing to be done, Fergus would be there to make sure it was not done until tomorrow. Today had already been put aside for a bit of not-to-strenuous relaxation. If a trot was required, Fergus would obdurately insist on walking. He was the ultimate definition of laid back, very self-assured in an aristocratic sort of way.

Both Chris and I were trying to find a way of handling home life without the riot of children wrecking our mental and physical equanimity. Fergus had it all worked out. We would be different people to those who had enjoyed the pleasure of Sam's company. We would be Fergus's people.

As in Brandy's early years, Fergus was now our family. For a while (before Dougal came along) Fergus was the third member of a threesome. That phase in life could have been difficult for Chris and me – it is for many couples. There was a complexity of emotions involved in coming to terms with the removal from our lives of what had been our mainstay since Kirkwelpington: the succession of children. Fergus was there for us and with his help, we came through fine.

Fergus turned out to be a huge character. He was always in charge, always Commander in Chief, doing what he wanted the way he wanted. Fergus expected the rest of the world to fit around him, including us. He was the most obstinate, difficult and self-willed of dogs and we loved him from the very start.

He took instruction as inappropriate to a person of his rank. Commands such as 'Sit!', 'Here!', 'Come on!' would all be met with a long hard look of disdain from under his bushy eyebrows which said, 'That is a most interesting suggestion. I will give it my consideration and will let you know my decision in due course.'

Fergus was thick-skinned, both physically and psychologically. He could be picked up by the skin on his back – hand-bagged – without protest. Injections bent the vet's needles. He would take a telling-off with serene equanimity; we could shout as much as we wanted, Fergus wasn't bovvered. The most reaction he would ever show to being reprimanded, by human or dog, was one of quiet reproach. *He* had done nothing wrong, what on earth was wrong with *us*?

The family remember Fergus as slow, which does not do him justice. Fergus was *considered*. If speed suited him, he had a fine turn of acceleration, disappearing in short order after rabbit, hare or deer. He had a special love of rabbit holes. He was fortunately too big to get down most, getting jammed a metre in which would necessitate him being extracted by his tail, which he did not mind.

When he was not yet fully grown, I had been entrusted with him while Chris was on some errand or other in Edinburgh and I decided on a nice long walk in the Pentland Hills. We were well into wilderness country when he took off after a rabbit. Frantic chasing after him ended up at the mouth of a large rabbit hole. No sign of Fergus! An ear to the hole revealed the sound of panting dog. He must deep down and well stuck.

Panic. Nobody knew where we were, we had no phone communication. I started digging with a stone, with my hands. He could not be left up there while I went for help. I would have to get him out by myself. Each inch gained toward him merely resulted in re-affirmation of his laboured breathing deep under ground. Then it stopped. Frantic, I dug all the harder – time was of the essence.

The panting renewed itself, but now close to my left ear.

There were now *two* of us digging our way deeper into the hole.

Fergus it was, come along to help, shifting soil at a great rate with his big paddy paws. It would seem that, having completed what it was that had been requiring his attention down the rabbit hole, Fergus had decided that he would now come to join me to give me a hand with my excavations. Even if he could not understand why on earth I was digging at that particular rabbit burrow!

Fergus was a hound. His instinct was to hunt and kill. When his blood was up he was seriously ferocious. He had once absented himself from the drive in the time it took us to go back into the house for the car keys. We found Fergus two doors down proudly carrying back to us a guinea pig from the hutch he had ripped apart. That the guinea pig in question had had a quick death did not do much to mollify our neighbour. It took years to make amends!

We missed a dinner party on his account. He was usually so slow, thinking about things, that the walk round the field was a gentle, refined affair. We had walked him just before we would be leaving him in the house while we were out. Then …

'Where's Fergus?'

Fergus was gone. Fergus was not minded to return to the call: that would have been below his dignity. We searched high and low, calling him in vain. We sought the help of neighbours. Fergus was lost and we were devastated. Three hours later he was found, sitting by the edge of a wood. He had eaten half the rabbit he had caught and was contemplating what might best be done with the other half. He had no intention of coming to our calls, nor of bringing himself home. He would however deign to wait, comfortably seated, full of rabbit, until somebody came along to pick him up. If they would be so kind!

Fergus was the same when he simply wandered a bit off route, or got left behind. Any normal dog would hear the call or whistle and catch up with their people. Not Fergus. He would just sit. Calling and whistling was a fruitless exercise, though he could hear us well enough. Did we really think that he, Fergus, would obey an instruction? Fergus thought rather not. We would have to go back and hunt around. Finally we would find him, sitting waiting, head up, asking us where we had been and what had kept us so long.

If only occasionally Fergus would bark! But never did. He did not go in for that sort of coarse behaviour.

*****

Fergus grew into a proud, self-assured, confident, big-boned, broad-headed, heavy dog of around twelve kilos. He had a wide jaw with big white teeth that were used only with the best of intentions. He was the gentlest and most forgiving of all the dogs we have ever known, a gentle gentleman. He never nipped, never bit, never growled, never got impatient with other dogs or with pesky grandchildren. The kids tugged and lugged him about. They would pull at his hair and grab him by the tail, they would lie on him for a warm pillow. He put up with it all with patience and equanimity. He loved the garden – not chasing balls (how undignified!), but lying in the sunshine, hour after hour, considering the world.

He was philosophical above all things. He expected us to be the same, expressing resigned regret when he found his mistress and master wanting – which was rather often.

Fergus did, however, have his peccadillos. There *were* indiscretions. He was good at eating stuff, all manner of stuff. This he would happily deliver up as a pile of vomit – usually in the middle of the night – all over his bed or (as he preferred) the soft-pile bedroom carpet.

Some of his culinary adventures were harder to shift. He was not to be trusted if one of the girls left their bedroom door open, and being teenagers, left their pants on the floor. Fergus could not resist girls' pants. He would chew them up and swallow them down. Then Fergus managed to avoid the vet by delivering the mangled fabric either through his back end (at which point he would invariably need quite a lot of help) or his front end (ditto). We got quite adept at pulling knickers out of Fergus.

Things that Fergus could not chew off and swallow down, like other dog's ears and the bottoms of people's trouser legs, Fergus would suck. His sucking was obviously a guilty habit of which he was a little embarrassed, for he would do it surreptitiously when nobody was looking, stealthily, so that trouser bottoms would be discovered at some later time mysteriously wet and shredded.

Fergus went about his day slowly, moderately. He was a quiet dog. He would not bark (standard wires never yap. They are not terriers, they are hounds). But he *would* sing. Fergus had a wonderful singing voice. He would be set off on any pretext, always in the mood for a sing-song. Fergus particularly liked to accompany his favourite tunes, which he did in time and in tune. Fergus' singing was both joyful and hilarious. He liked especially Copland's 'Fanfare for the Common Man', anything of Janáček, Border Festival Bands (he was great value on outdoor occasions when the bands were playing – onlookers were more taken by Fergus's fine singing voice than by the pipes and brass they had come to see). But the real winner was Mahler Five; upon hearing the opening chords, away he would go, smack on cue.

Other dogs were somewhat bemused by Fergus' singing. Later in his life, when Dougal was with him, Dougal would join in, wagging his tail with a look of puzzlement on his face as to why he was doing it at all. The two dogs singing in unison was a wonder to behold.

*****

Fergus shared much of his life with his sidekick, Dougal. Dougal joined Fergus's household in 2004 and he was there when Fergus died in 2014.

We had enjoyed our time with Fergus when we were just a threesome, especially in the first half of Fergus' long life when he was full of vigour. But he missed the company of other dogs.

Midge would come and go, and Fergus seemed to miss him when he wasn't here. Besides, we had been used to two dogs for most of the time since Brandy (not counting the cats, three horses, a cow, two goats, twelve hens, a score of sheep, numerous rabbits, bantams, hamsters, guinea pigs, fish and a canary). It wasn't as if a second dog would be any more tying!

First port of call was, naturally, the breeder in Holywell. She had had no more puppies since Fergus's litter and was giving things a rest. Starting again with the Kennel Club we tracked a breeder in the south Lake District. It was spring time, so we went down to look. The hawthorn was in bloom, it was a lovely sunny day and Fergus was not amused to be left in the back of the Land Rover while we went inside to inspect the litter. For wires the mother was quite smooth coated, she was also finer in build. The puppies were lovely (they all are!), and a little brindle male showed himself interested in us. So we brought him back home up to West Linton and The Small Hill. He was a happy chappy and Fergus took to the little fellow immediately, playing with him much as would an uncle with his young nephew.

The new addition was a diligent hard worker, anxious to take instruction and be a well-behaved dog. A sharp word was taken deeply to heart. He was the exact opposite to Fergus in other ways too. He was a sensitive soul, in mind and body.

Dougal (unlike Fergus) did not like to lie about in the sunshine (he was dark furred). The garden was for playing in, stealing plant pots and digging. He would bark at anything that disturbed the quiet. Knowing barking to be wrong, he would become suffused with guilt and slink back into the house, which he really didn't need to do.

Dougal's sensitivities permeated everything he did. He was always worried he had done wrong, in such contrast to Fergus!

He was easily upset by harsh words. He had thin skin in the other sense too; he hated his skin being grasped, yelping pathetically at any interference with his person. Wanting to be picked up was not his idea of being affectionate.

Dougal found it difficult to settle away from home – hotel stays were a nightmare for him. He was permanently on guard duty. Any noise would alert him to bark a warning to us that somebody was about to invade our space. As a result, with Dougal in the hotel room we never slept until everybody else had gone to bed. Then we would be woken up early next morning by Dougal warning us that the staff were arriving.

Dougal had an anxious life, always awaiting instruction, wanting to do well, go on errands, follow guidance. He was lightweight, quick in movement, alert to everything going on. He wanted to be busy. All very teckel.

The rabbits he would chase until, bemused, he was left with only a scent and a small round hole in the ground. While the rabbits were all good fun, the squirrels caused Dougal to be uncharacteristically infuriated. He could not abide squirrels. Any sighting would result in a furious chase. Dougal was incensed at the squirrel's predilection to cheat at sport by taking refuge up trees.

Fergus and Dougal did everything together; they were always with us as a pair and the bond between them was very close. The partnership however was one between senior and junior dog, the boss and the office boy.

The two of them would always go side-by-side. In hotels, coffee shops and bars they sat in each other's close company. An oldish man, dressed in tweeds, had been sitting at a table near us on the verandah of the cafe at Whinlatter, intently watching the two dogs – heavy-framed laid-back Fergus and busy lithe Dougal – their relationship clearly causing him some amusement: one coolly in control, the other alert and busy on guard detail. As he left to continue on his walk up the fell, he waved at the dogs and said to us,

'The Colonel … and … The Squaddie.'

Eh? … Oh … *Yes*!

*****

Chris and I had a happy decade as a foursome with the Colonel and the Squaddie.

The dogs were good with each other, and made such a pair that it often raised comment. Two proud dachshunds, bigger than anybody expected, tousled wire-haired, sturdy and alert, one flaming red, the other black. They were indeed a fine sight and we were proud of that. But that is not where our enjoyment lay. We enjoyed their being with us, good company, both good fun in their wholly different ways.

We went everywhere, did everything, very much as a quartet and it's there in all the family photos. I have one in front of me now. It sits on my desk right in my daily sightline. Chris is sitting on a rock in a nature reserve in Northern Ireland. Under her legs is Dougal, head up, looking out, keeping guard. At her feet is Fergus, lying relaxed, looking to camera; Chris is not (she never is). Chris is looking down at her dogs. It was ever so. Mother's dogs.

*****

As he aged, Fergus got slower and slower. All the rest of his character was there, for a good while anyway, he just got slower. The canters slowed to trots, the trots to walks, the walks to ambles. The rabbits were not chased, but watched, with moderate interest, as their white scuts disappeared into the long grass of The Small Hill.

In fairness, Fergus always had to travel twice as far as anybody else. Not because his legs were short, for they made up for that by being strong. It was because his legs went up and down, like pistons. So his stride, though active enough, was woefully short on forward momentum.

Fergus had always managed the longest of day hikes across mountain and moorland, and it was sad to see these powers diminish. Frustrating too, for the humans (and for Dougal) who would be out for a good brisk walk. For a little while we tried coupling Dougal and Fergus together, Fergus moderating the Squaddie's exuberance and Dougal giving his Colonel a bit of a tow. This worked to some extent, but only for a short while until Fergus got wise to the ruse and just sat down. He was much heavier than Dougal.

Fergus got to the point of dreading his daily walks; not just the longer middle of the day affair, but also (even) the early-morning walk up the hill with all its smells and excitements. Walks became a trial for everybody,

'Oh, Fergus! please get on! You are the most frustrating of dogs! Please move!'

It was something of a relief when it was decided that Fergus would be left on his bed while we went off. But it was the certain sign that decline to the inevitable could no longer be denied.

Fergus was coming up fifteen when his behaviour in the house took a turn for the worse with the onset of senility. He had always liked to lie against the radiator for warmth. But in his later years he would literally bake his head on it. If not head-baking he would be in the corner behind the door in the kitchen, staring vacantly into space. It would have been nice to imagine that in his mind he was chasing rabbits, but in truth, there was nothing there.

The final day came when the antibiotics that he was on were clearly failing to work. The vet was relieved that he would not be asked to go on treating a lost cause. He came over to the house and Fergus was put down in my arms on his rug, next to the radiator where he so loved to lie. It was a quite awful day.

Dougal, Chris and I were devastated. Fergus has now joined Midge under the oak tree in the garden. He loved the garden, quietly sitting in the sun for hours on end, just thinking about things, like any retired Colonel had every right to do. The little narcissus are there for him every spring.

Fergus, you were never a good dog. You were too wilful a character for that. But you were the gentlest and kindest person we have ever had the good fortune to know. You were stuffed to the brim with personality, you were much loved, and your life will always be part of ours.

*****

The house without Fergus was difficult for us to come to terms with. But Dougal, in his own quiet unassuming way, was there to share our misery, just like he shared everything with us, looking for nothing in return except our company.

Dougal was bereft at the loss of his Commanding Officer. Fergus and Dougal had been a double act and going solo did not come naturally to Dougal, but he made his pragmatic best of it, to become very special company for us.

Without Fergus, Dougal became more sensitive, more fragile, more in need of love. We had nobody else with us, so he got lots of that. Anyway, he was the easiest person to love. He was always quietly enthusiastic about everything, never over the top.

He rarely carried his tail high like Fergus (and Mungo, and now Rufus too). It would be halfway up – even when he was happy and confident. But, on the other hand, his tail rarely went between his legs unless he was really worried, such as when he was getting nasty taggles removed from under his armpits or between his toes.

Dougal was often 'not sure'.

'Not sure I was meant to bark there.' 'Maybe I'm a bit sorry about that. Not much sorry, but a bit sorry.'

'Not sure I'm meant to be on this chair.' 'But I think I'll stay here anyway.'

If it's a 'not sure' dachshund or a terrier, they usually yawn a couple of times, then decide that it was all good fun and do it over again. Quite soon.

Let it not be thought that Dougal, soft Squaddie that he may be, was a subservient or submissive dog (after all, it is the squaddies of this world that do the hard work). He was neither of those. He was a proud dachshund. He would defend his domain and defend his family, fiercely loyal to us. All threats were announced with warning woofs. He could be jealous too. With just the three of us, there was a certain rivalry between myself and Dougal for Chris's affection. The sofa was Chris and Dougal territory. Every evening they would be there together. Should I chance to join my wife on the sofa I would be given the eye and a low grumble,

'Mine! Not yours!'

But I would never move. There would be couple of yawns, then Dougal would simply put his head on Chris's lap and shun me by presenting his backside.

Because he was now our only dog, Dougal got dispensations that were never allowed to the dogs before (or after). Dougal started the habit of helping me cook. He would wait patiently at my feet for his titbit of a tiny piece of buttered bread, or fruit (he specially loved strawberry). Dougal was also allowed to come to my side at table (heaven forfend), to receive one (only one) bit of something or other from my plate. Dougal got privileges not afforded to others. It wasn't just that he was an only child now. It was that he never abused those privileges. Dougal never pestered, never persisted in his demands. He was, above all things, polite.

Dougal was a chatty dog. He asked nicely for things. There would be a deep woof if he was shut out or was where he didn't want to be. Though Dougal never lay in the sun out in the garden, he loved the sunshine coming into the house through our living room's south-east windows on any sunny morning. Dougal could smell sunshine, he loved it so much. He knew exactly where it would be in the house as the sun moved through its daytime course and would demand to be wherever it was. There he would be content, bang in the middle of any patch there was to be had. And if that patch was only small, then his head would be just there.

It is difficult to know why Dougal was so very important to us. Unlike Fergus, Dougal was unassuming. Maybe it was because we three spent all our days so close together, Dougal always there, always with us. His bed in our bedroom, his sofa in our sitting room, his house was our house.

He was with us every step of every daily walk around The Small Hill, every holiday, every walk into the hills. If we had to leave him it was briefly in the car. It was OK, it was *his* car; he was happy enough to curl up and wait for us.

*****

When Dougal got old it was hard for us to get used to the idea that maybe we should slow our pace a little for him. He was dragging a little, which I found deeply upsetting. I did not want Dougal to grow old faster than me.

Dougal walked with us to the very end; and it was a bitter end. We have a photo of that too, even after he had been so viciously mauled.

We had decided to go back to our favourite hotel in the Lake District because we knew Dougal was going very soon to leave us. We wanted him to have one more holiday. It started well but it did not end well. All because of an idiot dog-owner who fancied himself with his three big husky dogs.

Some weeks previous, Dougal had begun to pay unusual attention to one of his front paws. There was a growth and we bandaged it. Attired with a makeshift boot, Dougal got about fine and even came on the usual walks and expeditions up the hill. But it did not go away. This was not any abscess; it was cancerous. Dougal was over fourteen by now, and we knew his time was limited.

So, one last holiday.

We would take him to the Lakes, he was always specially happy to be with us there. The last day found us visiting what we thought was a garden, but actually turned out to be woodland. This misunderstanding mattered because I never would take my stick into a garden, but always would have my stick with me in the country. I did not have my stick.

Dougal had his paddy-paw bandaged and booted as usual. He was on the lead. Dougal had had poor sight for much of his life, and was by now quite blind. (For the past few months Dougal had always been on the lead, save for the house, garden and field, which he knew the way around well enough on his nose.)

We were on our way back to the car, when coming up in the opposite direction on a parallel path we saw a pack of three heavily built husky-style mutts pulling along on their leads an unshaven young man, oozing alpha male. By his side was his admiring girlfriend. He seemed full of the terrific impression that he and his fine dogs would be making on this old couple and their little black dachshund dog trotting on his lead.

Without warning, the pack went into full attack mode, barking and snarling, covering the ground between the paths in three bounds. They had wrenched free of their handler and we were defenceless. The dogs went for blind, vulnerable Dougal. He was bitten across his waist and thrown into the air to be bitten again before he could be rescued by my dragging him up with the lead to which he was still attached.

I gathered him into my arms, hoping that he might be just bruised but I knew it was worse. His thin skin was gashed open. The powerful jaws of the big dogs had closed on him.

We took him back to the hotel, stopping to get bandages and antiseptics for the flesh wounds.

Our state of shock and devastation was clearly justified the moment we got little Dougal out of the car. We were made sandwiches by the hotel's owner who had come to the door at our unexpected early re-appearance. A pot of tea arrived. We tried to make the wee dog comfortable but he was dreadfully unhappy, and confused by the pain. He lay distressed for the afternoon, but, good squaddie that he was, he came with us on one last little walk up the rise above the lake. None of us slept that night.

Next day we were home to the realisation that our little black blind friend had been irreparably damaged. He was put down lying in my arms on my lap. I was crying then, as I am crying now.

We buried wee Dougal, our wee Squaddie, still bandaged about his midriff and his fat paddy-paw, close by his old friend Fergus, his Colonel.

Those big dogs, or rather their owners, took from us not just our last dog, but our memories. Of the other dogs we can think back and smile. Happy days. Of Dougal all those joyful days (and there were many) are swept aside in tears, obliterated by the appalling events of his last day with us.

I'm sure Dougal will forgive them. Even if I don't.

*****

Chris and I vowed (again) we would never have another dog. It was all too raw, too painful.

We talked of how, in our dogless state, we could do things that we could not have done with dogs. We could have maybe some 'last holidays' ourselves. We could go to the Farmers Club in London and visit the West End theatres, the South Bank. We could go to those swish hotels that said 'No Dogs'. We could head off in aeroplanes to Italy, to Canada, to Spain. We could even go on a cruise. We were trying to comfort each other with such chatter.

We wanted none of these things and we knew it. What we wanted was Fergus and Dougal back. Our Colonel and our Squaddie.

Renewal – Rufus

Over the years our four children absorbed, unknowingly, the experiences of sharing their childhood home with dogs. They are infinitely the better for having done that. In turn they too have their families, their homes and their dogs. Life goes on. If the dogs are there to share in that, then all will be well.

Jo still has their two (now ageing) terriers; parsons, she will have you know – not *Jack Russells* – no, *parsons*. Emma, having lost dear Mungo, has a manic American coonhound in the family. (Not a *hound* – surely?) and a black Labrador pup – as if she wasn't busy enough already. Rebecca in Ireland has a pair of dotty Heinz (Oh dear). Our son Jon's family got through the Covid crisis with the help of none other than Rufus's year-younger full brother (a *daxy* – how sensible!)

Good fortune has smiled on us too. Perhaps the Fates thought to make amends for the cruelty they inflicted on Chris and me when we lost Dougal. For the line continues with Rufus.

Rufus it is who is now chasing around the hill, finding mice's nests, playing chicken with the sheep, smelling foxy smells. Rufus it is who takes his people for their walks in Scotland's Borders countryside.

*****

The last time our own household had been without a dog since I was a student was during that short gap between Brandy and Bella. And that was a *very* long time ago! With Dougal gone, we had an empty house, empty bedroom, empty sofa, empty walks, empty life, and we did not like it. Weeks went by. We did not get used to it. And, freed of the 'ties' of dog ownership, we definitely did not want to go on any cruise, nor to jet off to any foreign part.

Being miserable was not going to bring Fergus and Dougal back and we had never planned to be dog-less. The children and the grandchildren could not imagine us without a dog.

We got in touch with Mungo's breeder. Sometimes things go right. One of her standard wire bitches who was with a friend who lived south of Malton had just whelped and, she was *red*! Fergus-red.

A visit was arranged for four weeks later. We would treat ourselves to a stay at a Michelin Star restaurant – one that didn't accommodate dogs! We would go down, have a few days holiday in Yorkshire, choose our pup. It would be the reddest male in the bunch (the father was black). Rufus, big, strong, huge paddy-paws, confident, waggled out of the mass that was mum and nine pups, and came to say hello to us.

That'll be ours then. And that was that. We returned for him a month later.

Rufus is neither Fergus nor Dougal; he is Rufus. He has all the characteristics of a fine standard wire-haired dachshund. He is heavy built, brindled red, good-natured, people-loving, tolerant of unreasonable children. He has a fine sense of both humour and loyalty. Rufus is the only dog we have had who watches the television, taking an intense dislike to other dogs threatening to leap on us from out of the screen. He is not going to have uninvited guests in *his* house. He barks furiously at them – and it works every time.

The spot on the sofa next to his mistress is his territory of an evening, and should I choose to encroach, I get the eye:

'Hey, what you doing? You have your own chair!'

But I make him share it sometimes, and he seems alright with that.

Rufus is open-hearted and refreshingly naive. He wants to be friends with everybody. Those he specially likes are greeted with squeals of delight. He is a chatty dog, grumbling at us when we are not prompt with our preparations to take him up the hill, barking (*no barking, Rufus!*) with anticipation of a chase, or demanding his playtime.

He is with us all and every day. Those empty doggy spaces around the house, in the garden, up the field, are filled again to overflowing.

Rufus too seeks out the sunny areas in the house. He is awfully fond of buttered bread and strawberries. Next to charging about on The Small Hill, his favourite place is to lie in the garden, bathed in sunshine. There is nothing more comforting than watching a dog lying in the sun.

Rufus has the personality that is already making him into a very special dog. A fitting legacy.

*****

When Rebecca, our youngest and naughtiest, became a self-reliant, wilful, charming, teenager, our lives changed in a way that we were totally unprepared for at the time, though it must have been patently obvious to the dogs.

My life with dogs had started with the farm collies, terriers and hounds. They were part of the maelstrom of farm life, many of them with independent existences which slipped in and out of our childhoods almost by chance as each farm day sped by.

Then came the time of 'family dogs', starting with dear little Brandy. The family dogs were much more a bound-in part of Chris and my lives, integrated into the warp and weft of our family nucleus. They were not *alongside* that nucleus as the farm dogs had been, they were *inside* it, essential parts holding together the whole – parts without which, as we later learned, the 'family' did not properly exist.

Nonetheless, the family dogs had to take the rough and tumble of our lives as it came. They had to fit in with the other pets, the horses, the days away, the hikes long or short. The dogs' needs were accommodated much as those of the other animals about the place.

We defined our dogs. We asked them to put up with much, which they did, because they had no option. Then when our last child Rebecca began to make her independent way in life, there was a change, a change which, only now in our human dotage with Rufus, we have recognised for what it is.

It is our dogs which have come to define us! In old age, we have become their property, for them to look after, nurture and protect. As an animal behaviourist for at least a part of my professional life, I might have been expected to have some understanding of animals' ways – and so perhaps I have. But most clear in that regard is that Rufus understands infinitely more about his two charges – Chris and me – than we do about him! His world is deeper and more complex than ours, and has dimensions that are far beyond our comprehension.

He reads us. Most skilfully: our moods, our health, our actions, our *intentions*. He reads us with tolerance, humour and the sort of resigned love that a mother shows for her children. Rufus is dedicated to caring for the two stupid, ignorant people that he has been put in charge of. That is his karma and he seems to accept it with equanimity.

In the way that a couple who have lived long together tend in their aged years to fuse into one single entity, so Rufus has emerged, not just as a member of our little family, but as an integral part of ourselves – albeit somewhat wayward!

Our children, grown up and with their own children, are in their 'family dog' phase. They find it hard to see that Rufus is so much more than just 'the family dog'. One would not expect them (yet) to understand. But they will come to – if they are fortunate.

*****

As members of the village's 'retired' community, Chris and I came to meet – on our regular daily walks with Rufus – a number of 'fellow travellers' along that road that leads from the life of a recognised 'deferred-to' professional to that of inconspicuous non-entity. But we had our dog.

Rufus was always keen to say hello to whoever he might meet along the way. Just as the children at primary school were the social cement of our younger lives, so it is the dogs who have cemented the social interactions of our latter years. And we are by no means alone in that regard! It became evident that our identity in the community – an old couple with their companionable dog – was shared also by a good number of others in the village.

Of course there were young couples with dogs, and families with dogs. But these dogs were so evidently family add-ons. With us oldies, the dog is closely integrated into the family. Indeed, the dog becomes the family, the human family having flown the nest. It took a while to dawn on us how very different the role of the dogs in our lives has become over the long span of the years: from farm implement, hunting chum, house pet, children's friend, and at the last to play that vital part in creating that final chapter of the family home.

The dog's part in old people's last years becomes particularly poignant when, for those that we meet on the village green and exchange pleasantries, their dog is one part of a twosome. The dog then is the only thing in the world that many of the elderly have left to love and care for, and in return be loved and cared for by their dog.

Old Mrs Forbes was a regular. She would emerge from her cottage every day, oblivious to the weather, in the same clothes – heavy old coat, wellington boots. Her acknowledgement of the prevailing weather extended only to the position of the coat's hood: up or down. She would take her old dog on its daily constitutional, an hour every day, round the village lanes, the pair of them, slow walking, ambling happily about in each other's unquestioning company.

'He's getting on you know', she would tell us, as if she needed to be reminded of that fact herself, to get used to the idea.

'So are we all!' I would respond.

'Aye, I'm ninety-three.'

'Well, goodness,' would be my usual reply, 'You don't look a day over a hundred.'

'Aye … but the dog… Y'know, we always had a dog in our family. There's always been a dog. Often more 'an one. But always been a dog wi' me.'

One day she was there on the green without her big black Labrador.

'Where's your dog? Is he all right?'

'No. I've lost him. He just couldn't get out of his bed for me any more. He's gone.'

There was nothing to say. We did not want to leave her, standing alone on the river path, without her dog. We had never seen her without her dog and she looked strange … by herself. She must have sensed our thoughts.

Quietly, she said, 'I never realised that I was a person who lived alone till the dog was gone. Now I'm by meself. I know it now.'

'You must get another dog!' we said.

'Na, wouldn't be fair. I'm tae old. I'll not get anither.'

Mrs Forbes wandered off aimlessly back to her cottage. We never saw her out again. She had lost her reason to live.

*****

Covid lock-down might have had much to do with our and Rufus' mutual realisation that things between us three were going to be different.

Being in the 'vulnerable' age bracket, before the vaccine was rushed around the aged population with such audacious alacrity, we took self-isolation *very* seriously. We had to, but we also could afford to. We had the field, the hill. And we had the dog. The daily provisions came from the vegetable garden or in crates placed respectfully on the doorstep by kindly drivers who would receive our thanks at a distance of ten paces.

We filled much of the days in what turned out to be a rather nice spring and summer, with long slow walks amongst our wild flowers. And sitting surrounded by the splendour of nature now freed from the noise of aeroplanes and traffic, admiring the view in the sunshine, watching the dog playing and hunting in the long grass, listening to the birds, putting-up a pheasant or partridge, counting our blessings, and not much worried that the wet earth was seeping through our trousers.

Covid moulded the three of us into one. We had only each other, and we were pleased enough with that, and incredibly lucky to have the field in which to roam when others found themselves imprisoned.

*****

There is no doubt that Rufus, bless him, is, of all our dogs, the most empathetic toward ourselves. Of all our dogs he is the most sensitive when it comes to us. Why Rufus?

I think for that answer we must look not to him, so much as to ourselves. The extreme comparison is between Rufus as a fully paid-up member of our family household and those sheepdogs on the Welsh hill farms that I so admired in my youth. Those dogs were considered by the Dyffryn shepherd to be the tools of his trade. Clever tools to be sure, and ones with idiosyncratic natures that required him to adapt, a little, his handling of his tools. But at the end of the day, provided the dog did the job required of it, then all dogs were the same. Year on year.

Rufus tells us that they weren't. Those working dogs were as knowing as he is. It was the human who simply did not notice or care. In my early years studying animal behaviour it was emphasised that we must *not* consider the behaviour of our animal subjects in the same way as human subjects. That would be to anthropomorphise (to ascribe to an animal human-like characteristic and values) which was scientifically unprofessional and wrong. Some argue that our view of our dogs is no more than the construct that we have ourselves placed upon them. As an excuse for bad behaviour toward dogs it is convenient so to do; but it is also, as every person who has shared their lives with dogs knows, complete nonsense.

Dogs are their own individual, wonderful, knowing, feeling selves.

*****

Rufus shares with Fergus the character of the self-willed pragmatist. He has his own missions in life, and he is determined to pursue them. But when his people get in his way, or mean circumstance intervenes, he will be sorrowful, to be sure, but not for long. He will get over it and get on with it.

Rufus has soul.

Ah! The cynic will exclaim, beasts do not have souls – that is for humans alone. This I cannot accept. Not in stubbornness, but in the knowledge that I have come of late to realise that dogs have souls, and denial of this says more about mankind's ignorance and arrogance in not accepting this simple truth at the outset. But I have learned, thanks to Rufus.

Chris did not have to learn. She knew it all along. But then she never suffered years of scientific training!

Of course, when Rufus was a puppy, he was completely dependent on us for his well-being. And, naturally, he still is. He is not feral. But as Rufus reached adulthood, and as we reached dotage, a change has occurred, a reverse in who is carer and who is cared for.

Many years ago, when my son was developing an adventurous and free spirit, I found myself thrust into responsibilities that I had not bargained for. I was reluctantly drawn into the state of being the guardian of a teenager who was both more competent and more physically able than myself!

He would select alpine skiing pistes, cycle routes, highland munros to climb. I would toil to keep up, knowing that his safety was in my hands. Although, like every teenager, he knew himself to be invincible, it was me who had to be there to cover his back. I knew him to be vulnerable.

Carrying out my parental responsibilities towards an increasingly fit and dauntless young man became progressively onerous and often impossible until one magic moment toward the top of a Scottish mountain as the mists rolled in and I had no idea where we were or where we needed to go. It was my son who took to the map and compass and guided us down. On that mountain top the roles had been reversed. It was he, from then on, who shouldered the responsibilities, *he* who was to give *me* the lead. And so it has come to be the same for us two oldies and the young dog that is Rufus. And he takes his responsibilities very seriously, in his own dog's way.

*****

Even once we accept the depths of our dogs' psyche, at the end of the day, a good dog is still a dog that is good at being a *dog*. And dogs do doggy things. Wayward, naughty, irreverent, wilful things

Rufus' understanding of us is fascinating, but the delight that he himself is rests with the other side of his character, when he hunts amongst the long rough grass on the hill, lies in the sun in the garden, gets anxious on his walks if one of us does not keep up with the other, the Rufus that deigns to share his sofa of an evening.

The Rufus that welcomes us home.

Dogs' spaces

The farm dogs, like us boys, had their being in a countryside which was still largely untamed. I don't remember the farm dogs ever being on a lead – there was no need to resort to constraint apart from the cattle dog who was chained at the kennel on the yard so he was always instantly available (the others likely absent on self-appointed missions after rabbits, rats and the like). The farm dogs were free to roam their wide domain.

The family dogs find themselves more ambivalent about what territory is theirs. Family dogs must, necessarily, share their home with the family. They live not in fields but in rooms, rooms with doors, doors which shut. So instead of having for themselves their natural inheritance – the open countryside – the family dogs have only the bed on the floor of the kitchen, or a part of the sofa to call their own. And the collar and lead; that of course, is theirs to possess (lucky things!).

Our farm dogs owned the countryside. The farm fields, the ponds, hedges and woods, all were dogs' property. The farmyard too was dog property – to be cleared of the feral cats, the greedy pigeons, the bullying turkeys, the travelling salesmen sweeping in with their smart cars, eager to take an order. Dogs' duties were to be sure that every other beast on the farmyard knew exactly whose yard it was. The interlopers had to behave, do as the dogs were telling them, or else they would be herded off.

The fields were not for purposes of grazing cattle, the hedges and ditches not for draining the land, the woodlands not for providing fencing timber and fire fuel. These were for dogs to hunt and run and play in.

The wood on the farm was only some twelve acres, but it was packed with life. Every sort of bird's nest, in the bushes, the brambles and the scrub. At ground level were newts, stoats, weasels, red squirrels (the only sort there were then), ground-nesting birds, grass snakes, and (so we were told) adders. Above was territory for the loathed wood pigeons, the loved kestrels, the jays, the noisy rooks and the odd crow. The rooks made silly flat nests of twigs and branches, while the magpies built huge structures of exquisite engineering with fine roofs and cosy interiors. All birds' nests were there to be robbed: by the weasels, the avian predators, and by us boys. Wild bird egg-collecting was a serious pastime for all country boys.

The dogs would join in egg-hunting activities with enthusiasm, and regrettably no small degree of unnecessary clumsiness. The sheepdogs didn't like us climbing trees to the high nests, though. They would wait at the bottom, looking up, barking, telling us to 'come down at once'. Or maybe they thought we were up there to chase the squirrels down, with the objective of providing them with some sheepdog sport. The dogs hated the squirrels with a passion, mostly it seemed because the squirrels never played fair – chattering obscenities as they dashed up out of reach up trees whenever things were getting exciting for the pursuing dogs.

The terriers of course didn't much care if we were putting our lives and limbs on the line for the sake of a prized kestrel egg; they had their noses into the rabbit warrens and the fox earths. The foxes were considered a fair match for a good scrap, but the badgers, frankly, put fear and trembling into the terriers. The little dogs would feign ferocity by frantic barking at the entrance to the sett. However, in the event of brock being at home and none too pleased to have his daytime snooze disturbed, the brave rat-catchers would fall quiet and push off to find some less hazardous mischief to get up to in the undergrowth.

The farm was divided into fields of about ten acres. We had fourteen or so fields all divided by a hedge and ditch. A century or more earlier, the Irish navvies had come via Liverpool to dig out all the ditches. They were two paces wide and the same deep. On top of the mound of soil thrown out of the ditch, hawthorn was planted. Into the youthful hedge, self-sown native trees and shrubs including oak, elm, ash, sycamore, alder, blackthorn, cherry, rose, blackberry, honeysuckle, soon established themselves.

The ditches served their purpose to drain the wet land, so only the marl pits were left as open watery spaces. The hedges above the ditches were wildlife havens. The dogs would happily have spent their lives there – they were hotching with things to smell and chase. Best of all, they were well populated with naughty rabbits.

The rabbits were considered by the dogs to be respected game – they did not fly off, they did not run up trees. Why, they even had white scuts to help focus the chase. The terriers would flush the bunnies, then the sheepdogs and wolfhounds would take up the chase. The hapless rabbit would be gutted on the spot (extra treat for the victors), and the carcasses taken proudly home to Mother who would duly serve up a free and welcome casserole for supper.

Good dogs…very good dogs.

Before we abandoned the farm to its fate of being divided amongst the neighbours and the creditors, a last effort was made at achieving profitability. This entailed draining most of the remaining wet ponds, pulling out the hedges and making the fields three times bigger, for which the Government of the day gave us thanks in the form of monetary rewards, and the wildlife gave us no thanks at all.

All three, the people, the dogs, and the wildlife, pushed off and left.

*****

In the 1970s we took on The Small Hill by West Linton village in the Scottish Borders which has given such a joy to us and our dogs. We have tried to do something with the hill that might perhaps go some way to make amends for the rape of the farm.

That wee bit of hill is everything that the Cheshire farm was not. It is upland, populated with moorland grasses and wild flowers. At first it grazed the children's horses, fed the inhabitants of all too many rabbit burrows, while generating an ever-expanding population of docks, nettles, thistles and ragwort. But more recent years of nurture have helped nature take control of a more diverse habitat.

The invasive weeds fell to year-on-year scything. The rabbits were loved by the dogs, of course. Every morning was a rabbit chase, with the occasional capture. Though victories were few, they were sufficient to give the dogs daily excitement and agonising anticipation as they bounded up the bank to see what was over the rise by way of a fun pursuit.

The rabbits provided food for the raptors: the buzzards, the foxes, the stoats and weasels, a visiting sparrow hawk. But they really were too many, stripping the grasses and flowering native plants down to fine-mown lawn. We controlled the rabbits to manageable numbers (sufficient to amuse the dogs) by stuffing their holes with copious quantities of horse dung, of which there was no shortage! But in the end, it was the virus that has done for the rabbits, not the equine manure. The last dogs to really get into regular rabbit chasing were Sam (the retriever) and Fergus (our first wire-haired standard). For Dougal, and now Rufus, the bunny fun is all gone. And with them most but not all of the raptors.

I had fond hopes that the children's enjoyment of their horses would result in regular winter outings to follow the Borders foxhound packs, The Lauderdale and Buccleuch. It was not to be. Their cross-country jumping thrills were restricted to 'eventing'. Eighteen good jumps, to be sure, is as many as an average day's hunting might come up with, but there are no dogs – no foxhounds. 'Hunting with dogs' became illegal (on grounds of fox welfare) in the early 2000s.

The loss of the 'wild' hunting of foxes with hounds took the last remaining recreation out of my mother's old life. Hunting, for country folk, had nothing to do with the 'Field' following the hounds on their fine horses. Ordinary country people followed the foxhounds on foot. No way could they afford riding horses that could jump hedges and ditches, and clean clear a five-bar gate! Country folk turned out to the local hunt to see the hounds work the coverts and follow the scent of a fox gone away across the country – finding his track, wherever that might go.

But even though The Small Hill did not bring me back to my roots, it did, and still does, provide for the dogs a wild recreational haven. They love it, for the long grass hiding the skylark and pipit nests. For the grey squirrels which live in its boundary trees. For the smells of foraging fox or stoat. For the nests of vole, mouse (*there's a mouse! mouse!*) and shrew (*don't bite that, it'll have you and you won't like it*).

And, maybe especially, they love The Small Hill for its simple gift of space, the free space to run and run, to cavort, to roll in fresh dewed grass. They do not know to especially value their space, because it is there for them always and there is excess of it. The dogs owned by the village families, on the other hand, enjoy only the space that is the village green. For there it is that they are let off their lead to be followed by attentive owners clutching little black plastic poo bags.

The Small Hill that Rufus enjoys every day of his life is not quite the same as that which his predecessors romped in. Now it is husbanded for its natural-growing field flowers. These produce their own pleasures for Chris and me, and I daresay Rufus enjoys the scents of speedwell, yellow rattle, lady's bedstraw, orchid, birdsfoot trefoil, pignut, hawkbit and the like. But it's maybe not quite the riotous fun of a good rabbit hunt.

The modern way is all for 'wilding', but compared to the farm dogs, the village dogs have little of the 'wild'. The Small Hill has not, not yet anyway, been wilded. Neither has it had the 'wild flower sowing' treatment, because upland open grasslands do not suit invasive, foreign, commercial 'wild flower mixes'. It was just a matter of letting natural events take their course. Not interfering with the natural way of things by imposing aggressive farming practices such as cutting for silage, cropping for early hay, applying grass-encouraging fertilisers and so on. In the simple absence of discouragements, the wild flowers now give us a succession of delight from spring birdsfoot trefoil, summer orchids, through to the (rare) pasture *knautia arvensis* (Gypsy rose) of autumn.

It is not just us who love it. The dogs revel in the wildlife to which the native grasses and flowers give cover. Perhaps the grandchildren may take notice of what it is that makes people and dogs really happy. Which is the dogs having space to run and to hunt, and us having the privilege of watching them.